JAMIE OLIVER

7 WAYS

Photography LEVON BISS

Design JAMES VERITY at SUPERFANTASTIC

FLATIRON
BOOKS
NEW YORK

PAUL SMITH

I dedicate this book to Sir Paul Smith, one of the coolest, kindest creatives this country has ever produced. Thank you, Smithy, for being a guiding light to me and so many others. Love, J x

CONTENTS

EASY EVERYDAY IDEAS

7 Ways exists to give you new ideas for the ingredients you already know and love. Let's face it, life is busy, and these days we seem to have more and more demands on our time and our headspace. This book is about giving you solutions and breaking down any barriers you might be facing, while keeping things straightforward and giving you loads of inspiration on the food front for every day of the week.

18 HERO INGREDIENTS YOU KNOW & LOVE

For the first time, I've looked at the real data around what we're putting into our shopping baskets, week in, week out, and have built this book around 18 hero ingredients that just kept appearing. We know that everyone cooks the same small repertoire of recipes, so I want to help you expand on that and arm you with some new favorites. *7 Ways* is the most reader-focused cookbook I've ever written.

MAXIMUM FLAVOR WITH MINIMUM EFFORT

Over the last three years, wherever I go — parents' evenings, public engagements, random encounters on the street — I get asked when I'm going to write another *5 Ingredients*. It was the philosophy of that cookbook that really resonated with you guys, so I've tried to bottle that here. Think of it as the companion to *5 Ingredients* — once again we're keeping things simple, we're pushing maximum flavor with minimum effort, we want fun, and we want solid, super-tasty recipes that consistently deliver. That's exactly what you'll find in the pages that follow.

I'VE SET OUT TO GIVE YOU SOLUTIONS

We've got the same short ingredients lists backed up with a visual key, a range of portion sizes from solo meals to those for six, clear timings, lots of cheats and shortcuts and, ultimately, delicious recipes that work every time. I wanted to give you an even better experience than *5 Ingredients* here; one that answers even more of your needs. Whatever barriers you're facing – and I'm sure they're shared with other people – I've set out to give you the solutions in this book.

"I DON'T HAVE TIME"

Recipes range from just 10 minutes in total to slow-cook or one-pan beauties with minimal prep, where you can let the oven or stove do all the hard work for you.

"I'M BORED . . . I DON'T KNOW WHAT TO COOK . . . I'M STUCK IN A RUT"

With more than 120 recipes to choose from, whether you want something classic, comforting, light, hearty or slap-you-round-the-face exciting, I've got you covered.

"I CAN'T FIND FANCY INGREDIENTS . . . I DON'T WANT TO DO A BIG SHOP"

The majority of ingredients in this book will be easy to find in any food shop in any town in the country. You should be able to get stuff on your way home from work.

"I HATE WASHING UP"

Fear not, dear reader, I've got lots of traybakes and one-pan wonders in here that mean the clear down will be simple as pie. See page 11 for the lowdown.

"I DON'T KNOW HOW TO COOK"

Whether you're a total beginner or a kitchen ninja, these recipes will serve you well – they're concise, simple and, with a max of eight ingredients, not too much to handle.

"I WANT A TAKEAWAY"

If you really want one, go ahead, order one, but I've got loads of lovely fakeaways ready to tempt and delight you. Check out the bumper reference list on page 10.

RECIPES FOR WEEKDAYS & THE WEEKEND

Now, a quick note on nutrition. I want this book to be something you can pick up and cook from seven days of the week. With that in mind, 72% of the recipes are classed as everyday from a nutritional point of view, with 28% classed as occasional – think weekday versus weekend. Nutrition info is clearly displayed on every recipe page, allowing you to make informed decisions about what you're eating.

GET SHOPPING, GET ORGANIZED & GET STUCK IN!

I hope I've convinced you that this book deserves its rightful place on your kitchen shelf. This is exactly the kind of food I enjoy at home with my own family, and exactly the kind of food I hope you'll want to cook up every day for yourself and your loved ones. Have a flick through, get inspired, take a snap of your ingredients lists, get shopping, get organized, and get stuck in! I can't wait to see which recipes really tickle your fancy. Don't forget to tag your photos #JAMIES7WAYS so I can see what you're all up to. Have fun guys, and happy cooking!

MEALTIME INSPIRATION, FAST

The chapters in this book mirror our 18 hero ingredients; however, I know sometimes I m more in the mood for a certain type of food, so I've grouped some of my favorite genres together here.

FAKEAWAYS

ONE-PAN WONDERS

TRAYBAKES

SIMPLE PASTAS

BEAUTIFUL SALADS

SOUP & SANDWICHES

THE 7-WAY PANTRY

I've kept this to just five ingredients that I consider to be everyday staples. Cooking is simply impossible without these items at your fingertips, and I believe every household should have them in stock. Even though my own pantry is packed full of all sorts of things, it's these five that you'll see popping up regularly throughout the book and that you need in order to cook any of the recipes. They aren't included in each individual ingredients list as I'm presuming that you'll stock up before you start cooking. The five you need are olive oil for cooking, extra virgin olive oil for dressing and finishing dishes, red wine vinegar as a good all-rounder when it comes to acidity and balancing marinades, sauces and dressings, and, of course, sea salt and black pepper for seasoning. Get these and you're away!

THE FREEZER IS YOUR BEST FRIEND

For modern-day busy people, without doubt your freezer, if stocked correctly, is your closest ally. Whether it's preserving individual ingredients or keeping portions of batched recipes for future meals, food is brilliantly suspended, ready and waiting to help you out when you need it. And without stating the obvious, although this is still incredible technology, it's only as good as the food you put in it. If you're batch cooking, remember to let food cool thoroughly before freezing, breaking it down into portions so it cools quicker and you can get it into the freezer within 2 hours. Make sure everything is well wrapped, and labeled for future reference so you can avoid playing freezer roulette. Thaw in the fridge before use, and use within 48 hours. If you've frozen cooked food, don't freeze it again after reheating it.

LET'S CHAT EQUIPMENT

I've kept the equipment I've used here pretty simple – a set of saucepans and non-stick ovenproof frying pans, a grill pan and a shallow casserole pan, chopping boards, some sturdy roasting pans and a decent set of knives will see you through. If you want to save time, there are a few kitchen gadgets that will make your life a lot easier – things like a vegetable peeler, a box grater and a pestle and mortar are all fantastic for creating great texture and boosting flavor, and a blender and food processor will always be a bonus, especially if you're short on time! Recipes are tested in fan-assisted ovens. You can find conversions for conventional ovens, °C and gas online.

BE SHREWD ABOUT QUALITY

As is often the case in cooking, the success of the recipes comes down to the quality of the ingredients you use. There's not loads of stuff to buy for each recipe, so I'm hoping that will give you the excuse to trade up where you can, buying the best meat, fish or veggies you can find. Also, remember that shopping in season always allows your food to be more nutritious, more delicious and more affordable.

CELEBRATE CONDIMENTS

I use a lot of condiments in this book, like mango chutney, curry pastes, black bean and teriyaki sauces, miso and pesto. These are items you can find in all supermarkets, and of an extraordinary quality. They guarantee flavor and save hours of time in preparation. Most are non-perishable, which means you're not under pressure to use them too quickly. Over the years, the press have taken the piss out of me for using these so-called "cheat" ingredients, but I think cheat ingredients are great! They help keep food exciting.

BIG UP FRESH HERBS

Herbs are a gift to any cook. Instead of buying them, why not grow them yourself in the garden or in a pot on your windowsill? Herbs allow you to add single-minded flavor to a dish, without the need to over-season, which is good for everyone. They're also packed with all sorts of incredible qualities on the nutritional front – we like that.

MIXED VEGETABLE PACKS

I've used packages of mixed veg in this book. They're great because you get a variety in one happy parcel, meaning more flavor and hopefully less food waste. Note that some of the stir-fry packages contain beansprouts, which can't be eaten raw and need to be piping hot before you serve them.

MIGHTY MEAT & EGGS

Generally speaking, we should all be striving to eat more plant-based meals that hero veg, beans and pulses. If you are investing in meat, it makes complete sense to me to enjoy the benefits of better-quality organic, free-range or higher-welfare meat. There's no point in eating meat unless the animal was raised well, free to roam, displayed natural behaviors, and lived a healthy life. The same goes for eggs and anything containing egg, such as noodles and pasta – always choose free-range or organic.

FOCUSING ON FISH

If you eat fish, it's such an incredibly delicious source of protein, but literally the minute it's caught, it starts to deteriorate in freshness, so you want to buy and eat fish on the same day. I know that's not convenient for a lot of people, but I can only tell you the truth. If you can't use it that day, freeze it until you need it, or even buy quality frozen, canned or jarred fish, which can also be fantastic. Make sure you choose responsibly sourced wherever possible – look for the MSC logo, or talk to your fishmonger or the guys at the fish counter in your local supermarket and take their advice. Try to mix up your choices, choosing seasonal, sustainable options as they're available. If you can only find farmed fish, make sure you look for the ASC logo to ensure your fish is responsibly sourced.

DIAL UP YOUR DAIRY

With staple dairy products, like milk, yogurt and butter, please trade up to organic. Unlike meat, it is only slightly more expensive and I honestly couldn't recommend it enough – we're talking about pennies to upgrade. Plus, every time you buy organic, you vote for a much better food system that supports the highest standards of animal welfare where both cows and land are well looked after.

1 EASIEST BROCCOLI QUICHE
RED PESTO-LAYERED PHYLLO, CHEDDAR & COTTAGE CHEESE

2 ROASTED BROCCOLI ON ROMESCO
CREAMY LIMA BEANS, SMOKED ALMONDS, SARDINES & TOAST

3 CREAMY BROCCOLI RISOTTO
OOZY GORGONZOLA, ZINGY LEMON & VIBRANT PARSLEY OIL

4 BROCCOLI & HALLOUMI SALAD
SWEET SLOW-ROASTED CHERRY TOMATOES, GOLDEN PEACHES, MINT & GRAINS

5 BROCCOLI MINESTRONE
SWEET LEEKS, PANCETTA, ROSEMARY, PASTA, BEANS & PESTO

6 BROCCOLI & CHEESE PIEROGI
SUPER-QUICK SWEET CHERRY TOMATO & GARLIC SAUCE WITH CHIVES

7 SIMPLE BROCCOLI & TUNA PASTA
DRIED CHILI, SWEET GRILLED PEPPERS, BLACK OLIVES & PARMESAN

BROCCOLI

EASIEST BROCCOLI QUICHE

RED PESTO-LAYERED PHYLLO, CHEDDAR & COTTAGE CHEESE

SERVES 6 | **TOTAL 1 HOUR 20 MINUTES**

1 head of broccoli (13 oz)

6 large eggs

1 heaping teaspoon English mustard

10 oz cottage cheese

1¾ oz Cheddar cheese

3 tablespoons red pesto

9½ oz phyllo pastry

Preheat the oven to 350°F. For the filling, trim the tough end off the broccoli stalk. Coarsely grate the remaining stalk, then break the florets apart. Lightly beat the eggs in a bowl, add the mustard, cottage cheese and grated broccoli stalk, grate in the Cheddar, add a pinch of sea salt and black pepper and mix together.

Loosen the pesto with 3 tablespoons of water. Lay two sheets of pastry in an oiled loose-bottomed tart pan (10 inches wide, 1½ inches deep), overlapping them in the middle. Brush all over with some of the pesto mixture, then repeat the layers until you've used up all the pastry, brushing with pesto as you go. Roll and scrunch the phyllo in at the sides, like in the picture. Pour in the filling, then poke in the broccoli florets. Place on a baking sheet and cook at the bottom of the oven for 50 minutes, or until golden and set. Let it rest for 10 minutes before tucking in.

ENERGY	FAT	SAT FAT	PROTEIN	CARBS	SUGARS	SALT	FIBER
364kcal	17.8g	5.6g	22.6g	31.2g	4.8g	1.8g	4.6g

ROASTED BROCCOLI ON ROMESCO
CREAMY LIMA BEANS, SMOKED ALMONDS, SARDINES & TOAST

SERVES 4 | TOTAL 55 MINUTES

2 heads of broccoli (13 oz each)

4 cloves of garlic

1 x 16-oz jar of roasted red peppers

11 oz ripe mixed-color cherry
tomatoes

1¾ oz smoked almonds

2 x 15-oz cans of lima beans

5 slices of good sourdough bread

2 x 4-oz cans of sardines

Preheat the oven to 350°F. Trim the tough ends off the broccoli stalks, then halve each head and place in a roasting pan. Peel, finely slice and add the garlic, drain and tear in the peppers, then halve and add the cherry tomatoes. Toss with 1 tablespoon each of red wine vinegar and olive oil, and a pinch of sea salt and black pepper, then pull the broccoli halves to the top and roast for 40 minutes.

Meanwhile, crush half the almonds in a pestle and mortar. Pour the lima beans, juice and all, into a small pan and simmer on a medium-high heat for 10 to 15 minutes, or until the liquid has reduced. Remove the broccoli to a board, then pour the contents of the pan into a blender. Add the remaining almonds, tear in 1 slice of bread and blitz until smooth, then season to perfection with red wine vinegar, salt and pepper. Toast the rest of the bread. Divide the romesco sauce and beans between warm plates, and sit the roasted broccoli on top. Scatter over the crushed almonds, and serve with the sardines and hot toast on the side.

ENERGY	FAT	SAT FAT	PROTEIN	CARBS	SUGARS	SALT	FIBER
563kcal	20.9g	3.6g	39.1g	53.5g	11.8g	1.7g	17.3g

CREAMY BROCCOLI RISOTTO

OOZY GORGONZOLA, ZINGY LEMON & VIBRANT PARSLEY OIL

SERVES 4 | TOTAL 40 MINUTES

6 cups veg or chicken stock

1 head of broccoli (13 oz)

1 onion

2 anchovy fillets in oil

1½ cups risotto rice

½ a bunch of Italian parsley (½ oz)

1 lemon

2 oz Gorgonzola cheese

Bring the stock to a gentle simmer over a low heat. Trim the tough end off the broccoli stalk, cut the florets into small pieces and finely chop the remaining stalk. Peel and finely chop the onion, then place in a large high-sided pan on a medium heat, along with the chopped broccoli stalk and 1 tablespoon of olive oil. Cook for 10 minutes, or until softened, stirring regularly, then stir in the anchovies, followed by the rice to toast for 2 minutes. Add a ladleful of stock and wait until it's been fully absorbed before adding another, stirring constantly and adding ladlefuls of stock until the rice is cooked – it will need 16 to 18 minutes. Halfway through, stir in the broccoli florets. Meanwhile, tear the top leafy half of the parsley into a pestle and mortar and pound into a paste with a pinch of sea salt. Squeeze in half the lemon juice and muddle in 2 tablespoons of extra virgin olive oil.

Crumble most of the cheese into the risotto, squeeze in the remaining lemon juice, beat together, then season to perfection. Add an extra ladleful of stock to make it oozy, then turn the heat off. Cover and leave to relax for 2 minutes. Crumble over the remaining cheese, drizzle with the parsley oil and serve.

ENERGY	FAT	SAT FAT	PROTEIN	CARBS	SUGARS	SALT	FIBER
478kcal	16.5g	4.5g	15.8g	70.8g	4.9g	1.3g	5.8g

BROCCOLI & HALLOUMI SALAD
SWEET SLOW-ROASTED CHERRY TOMATOES, GOLDEN PEACHES, MINT & GRAINS

SERVES 4 | TOTAL 1 HOUR 10 MINUTES

11 oz ripe mixed-color cherry tomatoes

1 head of broccoli (13 oz)

1 x 15-oz can of peach halves in juice

3½ oz halloumi

2 x 8-oz packages of mixed cooked grains

8 mixed-color olives

½ a bunch of mint (½ oz)

4 tablespoons plain yogurt

Preheat the oven to 275°F. Halve the cherry tomatoes, toss with 1 tablespoon of olive oil and a pinch of sea salt and black pepper, and place cut-side up in a roasting pan. Roast low and slow for 1 hour, or until soft and sticky.

Meanwhile, trim the tough end off the broccoli stalk. Cut off the florets and cook in a pan of boiling water for 5 minutes, then drain. Use a vegetable peeler to very finely slice the remaining broccoli stalk. Mix 2 tablespoons each of peach juice, extra virgin olive oil and red wine vinegar, then toss half with the broccoli stalk. Put a large non-stick frying pan on a medium-high heat with the halloumi, drained peach halves and broccoli florets. Let it all get golden while you heat the grains according to the package instructions. Squash and pit the olives. On a serving platter, toss the grains with the remaining dressing. Arrange everything else on top, tearing up the halloumi and any large mint leaves, then spoon over the yogurt.

ENERGY	FAT	SAT FAT	PROTEIN	CARBS	SUGARS	SALT	FIBER
456kcal	20.9g	6.9g	17.2g	48.7g	13g	2g	9.2g

BROCCOLI MINESTRONE

SWEET LEEKS, PANCETTA, ROSEMARY, PASTA, BEANS & PESTO

SERVES 4 | TOTAL 40 MINUTES

4 slices of smoked pancetta or bacon

4 sprigs of rosemary

2 leeks

1 head of broccoli (13 oz)

5¼ oz random leftover dried pasta

1 x 15-oz can of mixed beans

6 cups veg or chicken stock

4 heaping teaspoons green pesto

Slice the pancetta, place it in a large cold casserole pan and put it on a medium heat. When it starts to sizzle, add 1 tablespoon of olive oil and strip in the rosemary leaves, stirring regularly. Trim the leeks, halve lengthways and wash, slice ½ inch thick and stir into the pan. Trim the tough end off the broccoli stalk. Coarsely grate the remaining stalk and stir into the pan, then reduce the heat to low and cook for 10 minutes, or until softened, stirring regularly. Cut the broccoli florets into small pieces and add to the pan with the pasta, pour in the beans (juice and all), then the stock. Bring to a boil, cover and simmer for 10 to 15 minutes. Season to perfection and divide between warm bowls, then dollop over the pesto and tuck in.

ENERGY	FAT	SAT FAT	PROTEIN	CARBS	SUGARS	SALT	FIBER
390kcal	15.9g	2.6g	18.4g	43.2g	5.2g	0.6g	7.9g

BROCCOLI & CHEESE PIEROGI
SUPER-QUICK SWEET CHERRY TOMATO & GARLIC SAUCE WITH CHIVES

SERVES 2 | TOTAL 50 MINUTES

heaping ¾ cup self-rising flour,
  plus extra for dusting

1 large egg

1 head of broccoli (13 oz)

1 oz Cheddar cheese

½ a bunch of chives (½ oz)

1 tablespoon sour cream

2 cloves of garlic

1 x 14-oz can of cherry tomatoes

Mix the flour and egg until you have a smooth dough, adding a splash of water, if needed. Knead on a flour-dusted surface for 2 minutes, then cover and pop into the fridge. Trim the tough end off the broccoli stalk. Remove the florets, halving any larger ones, and chop the remaining stalk into ¾-inch chunks. Put one-third of the florets aside, then cook the rest with the chopped stalk in a pan of boiling water for 8 minutes. Drain and mash well, then finely grate in the cheese, finely chop the chives and add half, stir in the sour cream, season to perfection and leave to cool. Peel and finely slice the garlic. Divide the dough into eight, then roll out each piece into a 6-inch circle, dusting with flour as you go. Divide up the filling on one side of each circle. Lightly brush the exposed pastry with water, then fold it over the filling, twisting along the edge to seal, like in the picture.

Put a large non-stick frying pan on a medium heat with ½ a tablespoon of olive oil, the pierogi and the reserved broccoli florets. Pour in ½ inch of boiling kettle water, cover and boil for 4 minutes. Uncover and fry the pierogi and broccoli on one side only for 4 minutes, or until the water has evaporated and the bases are golden. Meanwhile, put 1 teaspoon of oil and the garlic into the pan you used to boil your broccoli, stir until lightly golden, then pour in the tomatoes, simmer for 2 minutes and season to perfection. Serve it all together, sprinkled with the remaining chives.

ENERGY	FAT	SAT FAT	PROTEIN	CARBS	SUGARS	SALT	FIBER
402kcal	14.7g	5.5g	22.2g	48.4g	9.5g	1.5g	8.1g

SIMPLE BROCCOLI & TUNA PASTA
DRIED CHILI, SWEET GRILLED PEPPERS, BLACK OLIVES & PARMESAN

SERVES 4 | TOTAL 25 MINUTES

1 head of broccoli (13 oz)

4 cloves of garlic

½ teaspoon dried chili flakes

10 oz jarred mixed grilled peppers

8 black olives

10 oz dried fusilli pasta

1½ oz Parmesan cheese

1 x 5-oz can of solid tuna
in spring water

Trim the tough end off the broccoli stalk. Cut the florets into small pieces and finely chop the remaining stalk, putting it all into a large shallow casserole pan on a medium heat as you go, with 1 tablespoon of olive oil. Peel, finely slice and add the garlic, along with the chili flakes. Drain and tear in the peppers. Squash and pit the olives, tearing in the flesh. Cook for 10 minutes, stirring regularly.

Meanwhile, cook the pasta in a pan of boiling salted water according to the package instructions, then drain, reserving a cupful of starchy cooking water. Add the pasta to the broccoli pan, grate in most of the Parmesan and toss together, loosening with splashes of reserved cooking water. Drain and flake in the tuna, season to perfection, toss again, then finely grate over the remaining Parmesan and serve.

ENERGY	FAT	SAT FAT	PROTEIN	CARBS	SUGARS	SALT	FIBER
487kcal	17.4g	3.9g	26.1g	62.5g	5.3g	1.5g	5g

1 CAULIFLOWER REMOULADE
CRISPY-SKINNED CHICKEN, THYME, ONIONS & BAGUETTE

2 CAULIFLOWER CHEESE PASTA
CREAMY SAUCE, CRISPY GARLIC & CAULI LEAF BREADCRUMBS

3 CAULIFLOWER & CHICKPEA CURRY
COCONUT MILK, TOMATOES, QUICK HANDMADE FLATBREAD & MINT

4 CAULI CHICKEN POT PIE
SMOKED PANCETTA, SWEET CHERRY TOMATOES & PUFF PASTRY

5 HARISSA CAULIFLOWER TRAYBAKE
PEPPERS & TOMATOES, FLUFFY COUSCOUS & MINT-RIPPLED YOGURT

6 SPICED CAULIFLOWER RICE PIE
PAPPADAMS, ONIONS, FRESH CHILI, CILANTRO & YOGURT

7 CREAMY CAULIFLOWER RISOTTO
SILKY PROSCIUTTO, ROASTED CAULI, CRISPY THYME & PARMESAN

CAULIFLOWER

CAULIFLOWER REMOULADE

CRISPY-SKINNED CHICKEN, THYME, ONIONS & BAGUETTE

SERVES 2 | TOTAL 45 MINUTES

2 chicken legs

1 onion

½ a bunch of thyme (½ oz)

1¾ oz mixed baby cornichons
    & pickled onions

2 heaping tablespoons plain yogurt

1 teaspoon grainy mustard

½ a head of cauliflower (14 oz)

¼ of a good French baguette

Preheat the oven to 350°F. Put the chicken legs skin-side down in a snug-fitting non-stick ovenproof pan on a medium heat to crisp up. Peel the onion, slice into ½-inch-thick rounds, then add to the pan and fry for 10 minutes, stirring occasionally. Stir in the thyme sprigs and 2 tablespoons of red wine vinegar, flip the chicken so it's skin-side up, and roast it all for 30 minutes, basting halfway.

Meanwhile, finely chop the cornichons and pickled onions and place in a large bowl with 1 tablespoon of liquor from their jar, the yogurt and mustard. Mix well, then season to perfection. Very finely slice the cauliflower and any nice leaves, ideally on a mandolin (use the guard!), or coarsely grate it. Toss the cauliflower in the dressing to coat, then divide between your plates. Thickly slice the baguette and sit it on top of the chicken to crisp up for the last 10 minutes, then serve it all together.

ENERGY	FAT	SAT FAT	PROTEIN	CARBS	SUGARS	SALT	FIBER
534kcal	22.2g	6.5g	37.6g	48g	16.2g	1.3g	8g

CAULIFLOWER CHEESE PASTA

CREAMY SAUCE, CRISPY GARLIC & CAULI LEAF BREADCRUMBS

SERVES 4 | TOTAL 30 MINUTES

3½ oz stale sourdough bread

2 cloves of garlic

½ a head of cauliflower (14 oz)

1 onion

1⅔ cups reduced-fat (2%) milk

10 oz dried spaghetti

2½ oz Cheddar cheese

Tear the bread into a food processor. Peel and add the garlic, then tear in any nice leaves from your cauliflower. Add ½ a tablespoon of olive oil, blitz into fairly fine crumbs, then tip into a large non-stick frying pan on a medium heat. Cook for 15 minutes, or until golden and crisp, stirring occasionally. Meanwhile, peel the onion, then roughly chop with the cauliflower, stalk and all.

Tip the crispy crumbs into a bowl, returning the pan to the heat. Pour in the milk and add the chopped veg, bring just to a boil, then reduce the heat to low, cover and simmer. Alongside, cook the pasta in a pan of boiling salted water according to the package instructions. Just before the pasta is ready, carefully pour the cauliflower mixture into the processor (there's no need to wash it), grate in the cheese, blitz until super smooth, then season to perfection, and return to the pan. Drain the pasta, reserving a cupful of starchy cooking water. Toss the pasta through the sauce, loosening with a splash of reserved cooking water, if needed, then serve with the crispy crumbs, for sprinkling.

ENERGY	FAT	SAT FAT	PROTEIN	CARBS	SUGARS	SALT	FIBER
450kcal	11.5g	4.3g	18.9g	75.4g	8.8g	0.6g	5g

CAULIFLOWER & CHICKPEA CURRY

COCONUT MILK, TOMATOES, QUICK HANDMADE FLATBREAD & MINT

SERVES 6 | TOTAL 50 MINUTES

1 extra large head of cauliflower (2½ lbs)

2 heaping tablespoons korma curry paste

3 cups self-rising flour

2 x 15-oz cans of chickpeas

1 x 14-oz can of light coconut milk

1 lb ripe tomatoes

1 bunch of mint (1 oz)

1 heaping tablespoon mango chutney

Preheat the oven to 425°F. Cut the cauliflower into ½- to ¾-inch florets, finely slicing the stalk and any nice leaves, and chucking it all into a sturdy high-sided roasting pan as you go. Toss with the curry paste and 1 tablespoon of olive oil until evenly coated. Roast for 30 minutes, or until golden and gnarly. Meanwhile, pile the flour into a bowl, then gradually add ¾ cup + 5 teaspoons of water and mix into a dough. Knead on a flour-dusted surface for 2 minutes, then stretch it out to ½ inch thick, pressing all over with your fingertips to create dimples. Leave to rest.

Preheat the broiler to high. Transfer the cauliflower pan to a medium heat on the stove. Add all the chickpeas (with the juice from one can) and the coconut milk. Roughly chop and stir in the tomatoes and simmer for 10 minutes, stirring occasionally. Meanwhile, brush the dough with 1 tablespoon of oil and place directly on the bars of the oven to broil for 10 minutes, or until golden (keep an eye on it). Roughly chop the top leafy half of the mint (reserving a few small leaves), and stir through the curry with the mango chutney, then season to perfection. Serve with the remaining mint sprinkled on top and the flatbread on the side, for dunking.

ENERGY	FAT	SAT FAT	PROTEIN	CARBS	SUGARS	SALT	FIBER
500kcal	14g	5.1g	17.3g	77.1g	14.5g	1.7g	11.2g

CAULI CHICKEN POT PIE

SMOKED PANCETTA, SWEET CHERRY TOMATOES & PUFF PASTRY

SERVES 4 | TOTAL 50 MINUTES

1 head of cauliflower (1¾ lbs)	5½ oz ripe cherry tomatoes
1 red onion	1 heaping teaspoon grainy mustard
4 skinless boneless chicken thighs	2 heaping teaspoons liquid honey
4 slices of smoked pancetta or bacon	1 x 11-oz sheet of all-butter puff pastry (cold)

Preheat the oven to 425°F. Click off and discard only the tatty outer leaves from the cauliflower, then cut it into quarters. Blanch in a pan of boiling water for 5 minutes, then drain. Meanwhile, peel the onion and chop into sixths. Halve the chicken thighs. In an 11-inch non-stick ovenproof frying pan on a medium-high heat, fry the chicken and onion with 1 tablespoon of olive oil, a pinch of sea salt and lots of black pepper until lightly golden, stirring occasionally.

Add the cauliflower to the pan. Cook and turn for 5 minutes, then push it all to one side of the pan and add the pancetta to crisp up. Now add the tomatoes, mustard, honey and 1 tablespoon of red wine vinegar, and mix well. When it's looking really golden, roll the pastry out a little to fit the pan and place it over the top, using a wooden spoon to push it right into the edges. Bake for 25 minutes at the bottom of the oven, or until golden and puffed up. Using oven gloves, pop a large plate over the pan and confidently but very carefully turn out and serve.

ENERGY	FAT	SAT FAT	PROTEIN	CARBS	SUGARS	SALT	FIBER
615kcal	34.6g	16.9g	30.3g	45.7g	14.7g	1.4g	6.3g

HARISSA CAULIFLOWER TRAYBAKE

PEPPERS & TOMATOES, FLUFFY COUSCOUS & MINT-RIPPLED YOGURT

SERVES 4 | TOTAL 1 HOUR 20 MINUTES

1 head of cauliflower (1¾ lbs)	2 heaping tablespoons rose harissa
3 mixed-color peppers	2 cups couscous
14 oz ripe tomatoes	1 bunch of mint (1 oz)
1 bulb of garlic	8 tablespoons plain yogurt

Preheat the oven to 425°F. Click off and discard only the tatty outer leaves from the cauliflower, then cut it into quarters. Quarter the peppers and halve the tomatoes, removing and discarding the seeds. Break the unpeeled garlic bulb into cloves. Mix it all in a large sturdy roasting pan with 2 tablespoons each of olive oil and red wine vinegar, the harissa, a pinch of sea salt and black pepper and a good splash of water. Cover the pan tightly with aluminum foil, put it on a medium heat on the stove, and when it starts to sizzle, transfer it to the oven for 40 minutes.

Get the pan out of the oven, remove the foil, tilt the pan and spoon all the delicious juices into a little pitcher for later. Return the pan to the oven for 20 minutes, to get golden. Place the couscous in a bowl, add a pinch of salt and pepper, then just cover with boiling kettle water, and cover. Pick most of the mint leaves into a blender, blitz with 6 tablespoons of yogurt until smooth, then ripple it back through the remaining yogurt. Fluff up the couscous. Warm the reserved juices. Squeeze the soft garlic out of the skin. Serve it all together, sprinkled with mint leaves.

ENERGY	FAT	SAT FAT	PROTEIN	CARBS	SUGARS	SALT	FIBER
513kcal	14g	2.7g	18.9g	82.4g	19.2g	1.4g	10.8g

SPICED CAULIFLOWER RICE PIE

PAPPADAMS, ONIONS, FRESH CHILI, CILANTRO & YOGURT

SERVES 6 | TOTAL 45 MINUTES

2 onions

1 head of cauliflower (1¾ lbs)

3 tablespoons tikka curry paste

1 cup basmati rice

3 fresh mixed-color chilies

6 uncooked pappadams

1 bunch of cilantro (1 oz)

6 tablespoons plain yogurt

Peel and finely chop the onions, place in an 11-inch non-stick frying pan on a medium heat with 1 tablespoon of olive oil and a splash of water, and cook for 10 minutes, or until golden, stirring regularly. Cut the cauliflower into ¾-inch florets, finely slicing the stalk and any nice leaves. Stir into the pan with the curry paste and cook for 5 minutes. Pour in 1 cup of rice and 2 cups of boiling kettle water. Prick and add the whole chilies, then roughly snap in the pappadams and tear in most of the cilantro leaves. Stir well, season with sea salt and black pepper, cover and cook for 15 minutes on a medium-low heat.

After this time, the rice will have absorbed all the liquid. Uncover the pan, drizzle 3 tablespoons of oil around the edge and press down with a masher. Reduce to a low heat and cook for 5 more minutes to get a super-golden, thin crispy crust. Rest, covered, for 10 minutes, then loosen the edges with a spatula. Carefully turn the whole thing out onto a board or platter, then pick over the remaining cilantro leaves. Season the yogurt with black pepper, drizzle with a little extra virgin olive oil and serve on the side.

ENERGY	FAT	SAT FAT	PROTEIN	CARBS	SUGARS	SALT	FIBER
255kcal	13.1g	2.2g	7.4g	27.7g	7.5g	1g	4.4g

CREAMY CAULIFLOWER RISOTTO

SILKY PROSCIUTTO, ROASTED CAULI, CRISPY THYME & PARMESAN

SERVES 4 | TOTAL 45 MINUTES

1 onion	5 cups veg or chicken stock
1½ tablespoons unsalted butter	1¼ cups risotto rice
½ a head of cauliflower (14 oz)	1¾ oz Parmesan cheese
½ a bunch of thyme (½ oz)	4 slices of prosciutto

Preheat the oven to 400°F. Peel the onion, then blitz in a food processor until fine. Tip into a large casserole pan on a low heat with 1 tablespoon of olive oil and half the butter, stirring occasionally. Cut cute ½-inch florets off the cauliflower, toss with ½ a tablespoon of oil, spread across a baking sheet and roast for 20 minutes, stripping in the thyme leaves for the last 5 minutes. Chuck all the cauli offcuts, stalk and any nice leaves into the processor and blitz until fine.

Bring the stock to a gentle simmer over a low heat. Stir the rice and blitzed cauliflower into the onion pan, now on a medium heat, to toast for 2 minutes. Add a ladleful of stock and wait until it's been fully absorbed before adding another, stirring constantly and adding ladlefuls of stock until the rice is cooked – it will need 16 to 18 minutes. Add an extra ladleful of stock to make it oozy, finely grate in the Parmesan, then beat in the rest of the butter, season to perfection and turn the heat off. Cover and leave to relax for 2 minutes. Serve each portion sprinkled with roasted cauliflower and thyme leaves, draped with prosciutto, and with a drizzle of extra virgin olive oil, adding extra Parmesan, if you like.

ENERGY	FAT	SAT FAT	PROTEIN	CARBS	SUGARS	SALT	FIBER
449kcal	16.8g	6.9g	17.2g	61.1g	6.2g	2.5g	4.1g

1 AVOCADO HOLLANDAISE

STEAMED FLAKY WHITE FISH, ASPARAGUS & LEMON

2 AVOCADO PASTRY QUICHE

SWEET PEA, CHEDDAR & BASIL FILLING, MIXED GARDEN LEAVES

3 AVOCADO TEMPURA

SWEET PEPPER & ROSE HARISSA DIPPING SAUCE

4 AVOCADO & CHICKPEA TOASTIE

WARMING SPICED HARISSA & COOLING COTTAGE CHEESE & PARMESAN

5 AVOCADO CAESAR

ULTIMATE BREADCRUMBS, CRUNCHY LETTUCE & SHAVED PARMESAN

6 BEAUTIFUL BAKED AVOCADO

STUFFED WITH CREAMY CHEESY SHRIMP ON A BED OF TOMATOES

7 AVO QUESADILLAS

RED LEICESTER CHEESE, SWEET PEPPERS & AVO SALSA

AVOCADO

AVOCADO HOLLANDAISE
STEAMED FLAKY WHITE FISH, ASPARAGUS & LEMON

SERVES 2 | TOTAL 15 MINUTES

1 bunch of thick asparagus (12 oz)

2 x 5¼-oz chunky fillets of white fish, skin off, pin-boned

2 scallions

1 lemon

½ a bunch of tarragon (½ oz)

1 really ripe avocado

1 large egg

Pour ½ inch of water into a large cold pan. Snap the woody ends off the asparagus, then place the spears in the pan and sit the fish fillets on top. Place on a high heat, cover and steam for 5 minutes, or until the fish is just cooked through. Meanwhile, trim the scallions, roughly chop the green parts and place in a small pan on a high heat with half the lemon juice, 1 teaspoon of red wine vinegar, a pinch of sea salt and black pepper and 7 tablespoons of water. Bring to a boil while you pick half the tarragon leaves into a blender. Halve and pit the avocado, scoop the flesh into the blender and add just the egg yolk. Pour in the hot scallion mixture, then blitz until silky smooth and season to perfection. Very finely slice the whites of the scallions and mix with the remaining tarragon leaves.

Serve the fish and asparagus with the avocado hollandaise, finishing with pinches of the tarragon and scallion and a light drizzle of extra virgin olive oil. Serve with lemon wedges, for squeezing over.

ENERGY	FAT	SAT FAT	PROTEIN	CARBS	SUGARS	SALT	FIBER
304kcal	15.5g	3.4g	35.8g	5.3g	4.1g	0.8g	1.9g

AVOCADO PASTRY QUICHE

SWEET PEA, CHEDDAR & BASIL FILLING, MIXED GARDEN LEAVES

SERVES 6 | TOTAL 1 HOUR

2 ripe avocados

3¼ cups self-rising flour,
    plus extra for dusting

6 large eggs

10 oz frozen peas

3 oz Cheddar cheese

½ a bunch of basil (½ oz)

3½-oz package of mixed salad

1 lemon

Halve, pit and peel the avocados. Weigh the flesh – you want 7 oz to get your ratios right (if you don't have enough, simply top up to 7 oz with extra virgin olive oil). In a large bowl, smash up the avo, then gradually rub in the flour and ¼ cup of cold water until you have a dough. Knead until smooth, then wrap and rest for 15 minutes. For the filling, crack the eggs into a blender, then add the frozen peas and most of the Cheddar. Rip in the top leafy half of the basil, add a pinch of sea salt and black pepper, and blitz until smooth.

Preheat the oven to 400°F. Roll out the avocado pastry on a flour-dusted surface to just under ¼ inch thick. Loosely roll it up around the rolling pin, then unroll it over an oiled 14- x 10-inch rimmed baking sheet, ease it into the sides and prick the base. Roughly tear off any big bits of overhang, then bake for 10 minutes, or until lightly golden. Evenly pour in the filling and bake for another 15 minutes, or until set, then finely grate over the remaining cheese. Dress the salad leaves with extra virgin olive oil and lemon juice, season, then sprinkle over the quiche to serve.

ENERGY	FAT	SAT FAT	PROTEIN	CARBS	SUGARS	SALT	FIBER
764kcal	52.6g	11.3g	21g	55.9g	2.4g	1.1g	4.9g

AVOCADO TEMPURA

SWEET PEPPER & ROSE HARISSA DIPPING SAUCE

SERVES 2 | **TOTAL 20 MINUTES**

⅔ cup rice flour	4 scallions
3½ oz jarred roasted red peppers	1 large ripe avocado
2 teaspoons rose harissa	4 sprigs of Italian parsley
2 tablespoons plain yogurt	1 lime

In a bowl, whisk the flour with a pinch of sea salt and ⅔ cup of water until you have a smooth batter. In a blender, blitz the drained peppers with the harissa and half the yogurt until smooth, then season to perfection. Trim and halve the scallions. Halve and pit the avocado, use a spoon to scoop the halves out of the skins, then cut each half into four wedges.

Place a large sturdy pan on a high heat with ¾ inch of olive oil. Use a thermometer to tell when it's ready (350°F), or add a scallion trimming and wait until it turns golden – that's the sign it's good to go. One by one, dip the avocado, scallions and parsley into the batter and, letting any excess drip off, place gently in the oil, turning with tongs when golden. Remove to paper towel to drain well, then serve sprinkled with a little salt. Ripple the remaining yogurt through the pepper mixture, for dipping, and serve with lime wedges, for squeezing over.

ENERGY	FAT	SAT FAT	PROTEIN	CARBS	SUGARS	SALT	FIBER
487kcal	30.7g	5.5g	6g	45g	4g	1g	1.8g

AVOCADO & CHICKPEA TOASTIE

WARMING SPICED HARISSA & COOLING COTTAGE CHEESE & PARMESAN

SERVES 2 | TOTAL 25 MINUTES

1 large ripe avocado

½ oz Parmesan cheese

2 slices of brown bread

2 heaping teaspoons rose harissa,
   plus extra to serve

2 heaping tablespoons cottage cheese

2 heaping tablespoons drained
   jarred chickpeas

This recipe is completely bonkers but, trust me, it's utterly delicious. Turn the broiler on to high. Halve and pit the avocado, then scoop the flesh onto a board. Finely grate over the Parmesan and smash with a fork until super smooth, then season to perfection with sea salt and black pepper. Lightly toast the bread.

Spread each piece of toast, from corner to corner, with the harissa, then spoon the cottage cheese into the center. Use a knife to spread the avocado over the cottage cheese and all of the toast, nice and high, then poke in the chickpeas. Place on a baking sheet, drizzle with 1 teaspoon of olive oil and pop under the broiler for 10 to 15 minutes, or until lightly golden. Drizzle with extra harissa, to serve.

ENERGY	FAT	SAT FAT	PROTEIN	CARBS	SUGARS	SALT	FIBER
424kcal	22.1g	5.9g	19.4g	35.5g	3.6g	0.9g	8.6g

AVOCADO CAESAR

ULTIMATE BREADCRUMBS, CRUNCHY LETTUCE & SHAVED PARMESAN

SERVES 4 | TOTAL 20 MINUTES

3 oz garlic bread

4 anchovy fillets in oil

2 romaine lettuces

¼ cup plain yogurt

1 heaping teaspoon Dijon mustard

1 tablespoon Worcestershire sauce

2 ripe avocados

1 oz Parmesan cheese

Tear the garlic bread into a food processor, add the anchovies, then blitz into coarse even-sized crumbs. Pour into a large non-stick frying pan on a medium heat and toast until beautifully golden, tossing regularly.

Meanwhile, wash the lettuces, click off 5 outer leaves and tear them into the processor. Add the yogurt, mustard, Worcestershire sauce and 1 tablespoon of red wine vinegar. Halve and pit the avocados, and scoop one avocado half into the processor. Blitz into a smooth dressing, then season to perfection. Slice the remaining lettuce and arrange over a large platter, then spoon over the dressing. Slice the rest of the avo. Shave the Parmesan with a vegetable peeler. Sprinkle the hot crispy crumbs over the platter, then finish with the sliced avo and Parmesan.

ENERGY	FAT	SAT FAT	PROTEIN	CARBS	SUGARS	SALT	FIBER
241kcal	16.9g	5.9g	8.6g	14.5g	5g	1.3g	2.4g

BEAUTIFUL BAKED AVOCADO

STUFFED WITH CREAMY CHEESY SHRIMP ON A BED OF TOMATOES

SERVES 4 | TOTAL 25 MINUTES

1 lb ripe mixed-color tomatoes

2 ripe avocados

2 oz Cheddar cheese

7 tablespoons reduced-fat crème fraîche

5¼ oz small cooked peeled shrimp

cayenne pepper

4 slices of good sourdough bread

Preheat the oven to 400°F. Slice the tomatoes ¼ inch thick, and arrange them nicely in a 12-inch non-stick ovenproof frying pan. Drizzle with 1 tablespoon of olive oil and a pinch of sea salt and black pepper. Halve and pit the avocados, then use a spoon to scoop the halves out of the skins. Place on the tomatoes. Finely grate most of the cheese into a bowl, then mix with the crème fraîche and shrimp.

Divide the creamy shrimp mixture between the avo halves. Finely grate over the remaining cheese and sprinkle with a pinch of cayenne. Bake for 15 minutes, or until golden and bubbling. Toast the bread, ready to mop up the juices.

ENERGY	FAT	SAT FAT	PROTEIN	CARBS	SUGARS	SALT	FIBER
369kcal	22.9g	8.7g	16.9g	23.5g	5.6g	1.4g	1.3g

AVO QUESADILLAS

RED LEICESTER CHEESE, SWEET PEPPERS & AVO SALSA

SERVES 2 | TOTAL 30 MINUTES

2 mixed-color peppers

½ a bunch of mint (½ oz)

1¾ oz red Leicester cheese or other
   English Cheddar

2 large whole-grain tortillas

1 ripe avocado

2 limes

¼ cup plain yogurt

2 teaspoons chipotle hot sauce

Blacken the whole peppers over a direct flame on the stove, or in a grill pan on a high heat, until charred all over, while you pick the mint leaves and finely chop half of them. Pop the peppers into a bowl, cover and leave for 10 minutes, then scrape off most of the skin, seed and chop into ½-inch dice. Mix with 1 tablespoon of red wine vinegar and the chopped mint, then season to perfection. Coarsely grate half the cheese over one tortilla, scatter over the peppers, grate over the rest of the cheese, then put the other tortilla on top and press down. Put a large non-stick frying pan on a medium heat, carefully lift in the tortillas and toast for 4 minutes on each side, or until golden and the cheese has melted.

Meanwhile, halve and pit the avocado, and scoop one avocado half into a blender with the remaining mint leaves, the juice of 1 lime, 3 tablespoons of yogurt and 2 tablespoons of water. Blitz until smooth, then season to perfection. Divide between your plates, ripple through the remaining yogurt and the hot sauce, then slice and divide up the remaining avo. Serve with wedges of quesadilla, for dunking, and lime wedges, for squeezing over.

ENERGY	FAT	SAT FAT	PROTEIN	CARBS	SUGARS	SALT	FIBER
440kcal	23.1g	9.7g	16.2g	39.5g	11.5g	1.1g	8.9g

1 SPEEDY CHICKEN & CHORIZO
TOMATO & OREGANO GARLICKY TOASTS, ARUGULA & LEMON

2 PHYLLO CHICKEN KIEV
SWEET PEA & POTATO MASH, BROCCOLINI

3 MY KINDA BUTTER CHICKEN
FRAGRANT SPICES, TOMATOES, CASHEW BUTTER & YOGURT

4 JERK SPICED CHICKEN IN A BUN
CREAMY SLAW, CHARRED PINEAPPLE & PICKLED SCOTCH BONNET CHILI

5 SWEET CHILI CHICKEN BALLS
CRUNCHY MIXED VEG & EGG-FRIED RICE, SOY, GINGER & CILANTRO

6 CRISPY GOLDEN CHICKEN
CRUNCHY BACON BREADCRUMBS, AVO & CHILI SAUCE

7 CHICKEN NOODLE SOUP
GINGER, RENDANG SPICE, CRUNCHY VEG & COCONUT MILK

CHICKEN

BREAST

SPEEDY CHICKEN & CHORIZO

TOMATO & OREGANO GARLICKY TOASTS, ARUGULA & LEMON

SERVES 2 | TOTAL 20 MINUTES

5½ oz ripe mixed-color cherry tomatoes

2 teaspoons dried oregano, ideally the flowering kind

½ a good French baguette

2 x 5¼-oz skinless boneless chicken breasts

1¾ oz chorizo

1 clove of garlic

½ a lemon

¾ oz arugula

Quarter or slice the tomatoes, then mix with the oregano, 1 tablespoon each of red wine vinegar and extra virgin olive oil and a pinch of sea salt and black pepper. Cut the baguette into ¾-inch-thick slices and toast in a large non-stick frying pan on a high heat until golden. Meanwhile, lightly score the chicken breasts on one side, then place between two sheets of parchment paper and bash and flatten to ½ inch thick with a rolling pin, or the bottom of a pan. Finely slice the chorizo.

Remove the toasts when golden and cook the chorizo in the pan for 1 minute, then add the chicken and fry for 6 minutes, or until golden and cooked through, turning halfway and sitting the chorizo on top of the chicken once crispy. Season with black pepper. Peel and halve the garlic clove and rub over the toasts. Finely slice the garlic and sprinkle into the chicken pan for the last couple of minutes to get golden. Pile the dressed tomatoes and juices onto the toasts with the lemon-dressed arugula. Slice the chicken and serve alongside, sprinkled with the crispy chorizo and garlic.

ENERGY	FAT	SAT FAT	PROTEIN	CARBS	SUGARS	SALT	FIBER
444kcal	16.1g	4.4g	46.2g	30.4g	5.2g	1.6g	3g

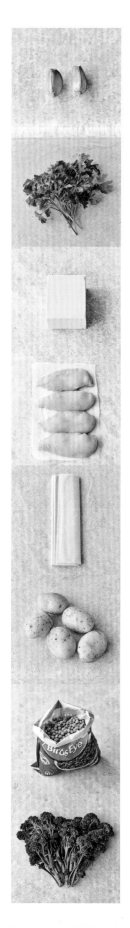

PHYLLO CHICKEN KIEV
SWEET PEA & POTATO MASH, BROCCOLINI

SERVES 4 | **TOTAL 45 MINUTES**

2 cloves of garlic

1 bunch of Italian parsley (1 oz)

1 oz soft unsalted butter

4 x 5¼-oz skinless boneless
chicken breasts

4 sheets of phyllo pastry

1¾ lbs potatoes

14 oz frozen peas

7 oz purple broccolini

Preheat the oven to 400°F. Peel and finely grate the garlic, finely chop the parsley, stalks and all, then mix both with the soft butter and season with sea salt and black pepper. Use the tip of a sharp knife to slice into the thickest part of each chicken breast and create a pocket. Divide and stuff in the garlic butter, then shape the breasts back into their original form, sealing the butter inside. Gather up one sheet of phyllo in waves and wrap around one breast. Repeat, lining up the kievs on a large oiled rimmed baking sheet. Mix 1 tablespoon of olive oil with 1 teaspoon of red wine vinegar, then lightly brush the phyllo, reserving the remaining mixture for later. Roast at the bottom of the oven for 25 minutes, or until golden, juicy and cooked through.

Meanwhile, peel the potatoes, chop into even-sized chunks and cook in a large pan of boiling salted water for 15 minutes, or until tender, adding the peas for the last 2 minutes. Trim the tough ends off the broccolini stalks, halve any thicker stalks lengthways, toss with the remaining oil and vinegar mixture and add to the chicken pan for the last 10 minutes. Drain the potatoes and peas, then mash with 1 teaspoon of extra virgin olive oil and season to perfection. Serve it all together.

ENERGY	FAT	SAT FAT	PROTEIN	CARBS	SUGARS	SALT	FIBER
561kcal	16.1g	5.7g	49.2g	58g	5.6g	1g	10.2g

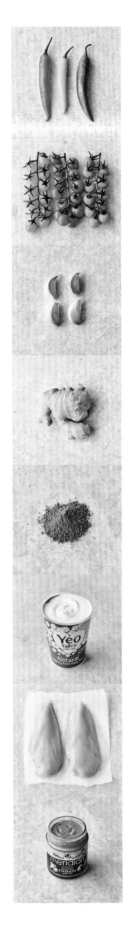

MY KINDA BUTTER CHICKEN

FRAGRANT SPICES, TOMATOES, CASHEW BUTTER & YOGURT

SERVES 2 | **TOTAL 40 MINUTES**

2–3 fresh mixed-color chilies

12 oz ripe mixed-color cherry
    tomatoes

4 cloves of garlic

2½-inch piece of fresh ginger

1 tablespoon garam masala

4 heaping tablespoons plain yogurt

2 x 5¼-oz skinless boneless
    chicken breasts

2 tablespoons smooth cashew butter

Halve and seed the chilies. Place in a large non-stick frying pan on a high heat with the tomatoes and blacken all over, turning occasionally. Meanwhile, peel the garlic and ginger, and finely grate into a large bowl. Add most of the garam masala, a pinch of sea salt and black pepper and 1 tablespoon of yogurt. Deeply score the chicken breasts at ½-inch intervals, then massage with the marinade.

Once charred, remove the tomatoes and chilies to a board, returning the pan to a medium heat with ½ a tablespoon of olive oil and the chicken. Cook and char for 10 minutes, turning halfway, while you pinch off and discard the tomato skins and roughly chop 1–2 of the chilies, to taste. Remove the gnarly chicken from the pan and go in with the tomatoes, chopped chilies and cashew butter. Pour in 1 cup of boiling kettle water and stir to pick up the sticky bits. Let it bubble vigorously for 2 minutes and once it starts to thicken, return the chicken to the pan, turning in the sauce for a final 2 minutes, or until cooked through, then remove to a board. Off the heat, season the sauce to perfection, then ripple through the remaining yogurt. Slice the chicken and serve with the remaining chili and garam masala.

ENERGY	FAT	SAT FAT	PROTEIN	CARBS	SUGARS	SALT	FIBER
435kcal	20.7g	4.8g	45.2g	17.5g	11.1g	0.8g	3.4g

JERK SPICED CHICKEN IN A BUN

CREAMY SLAW, CHARRED PINEAPPLE & PICKLED SCOTCH BONNET CHILI

SERVES 2 | **TOTAL 15 MINUTES**

1 fresh Scotch bonnet or red chili

1 x 5¼-oz skinless boneless
   chicken breast

1 heaping teaspoon jerk seasoning,
   plus extra for sprinkling

1 x 8-oz can of pineapple rings in juice

1 carrot

¼ of a green cabbage (5¼ oz)

2 heaping tablespoons plain yogurt

2 large soft buns

Halve, seed and finely slice the Scotch bonnet chili, place it in a sieve and run cold water over it to start softening the kick. Put a grill pan or large non-stick frying pan on a high heat. Carefully cut the chicken breast in half through the middle to give you two thin flat pieces. Toss them with the jerk seasoning and 1 tablespoon of olive oil until well coated. Cook the chicken in the hot pan for 5 minutes, turning halfway. Char the pineapple rings alongside, reserving the juice.

Put the pineapple juice and chili in a bowl and mix with a small pinch of sea salt and 1 tablespoon of red wine vinegar. Scrub the carrot, then coarsely grate with the cabbage. Mix the veg with the yogurt and a splash of liquor from the chili, then season to perfection to make a slaw. Stack the chicken and pineapple on one side of the pan, then halve and quickly toast the buns. Halve the cooked chicken and layer up in the buns with the slaw, pineapple, a little pickled chili (it's hot!) and an extra sprinkling of jerk seasoning. Pat, squeeze and enjoy.

ENERGY	FAT	SAT FAT	PROTEIN	CARBS	SUGARS	SALT	FIBER
505kcal	12.5g	3.1g	31g	71.2g	24.3g	1.6g	6.3g

SWEET CHILI CHICKEN BALLS

CRUNCHY MIXED VEG & EGG-FRIED RICE, SOY, GINGER & CILANTRO

SERVES 2 | TOTAL 20 MINUTES

1½-inch piece of fresh ginger

½ a bunch of cilantro (½ oz)

1 x 5¼-oz skinless boneless
   chicken breast

2 tablespoons sweet chili sauce

1 x 8-oz package of cooked rice

10-oz package of mixed stir-fry veg

2 large eggs

1 tablespoon reduced-sodium
   soy sauce

Peel the ginger. Pick half the cilantro leaves and put aside, then finely chop the rest, stalks and all, with the ginger. Add the chicken breast to the board, then chop and mix until you have a fine mince-type consistency. With wet hands, divide into eight, and roll into balls. Place in an 8-inch non-stick frying pan on a medium-high heat with ½ a tablespoon of olive oil. Fry for 4 minutes, tossing regularly, then add the sweet chili sauce to glaze for another 2 minutes. Meanwhile, put a large non-stick frying pan on a medium heat alongside, go in with ½ a tablespoon of oil, the rice and mixed veg. Toss regularly while the balls cook.

Beat the eggs and divide between the pans, tossing into the veg and rice but letting the egg flow around the balls and set as it cooks. Mix the soy into the egg-fried rice to season it to taste, then serve on a platter, sliding your silky omelet and chicken balls on top. Finish with the reserved cilantro leaves.

ENERGY	FAT	SAT FAT	PROTEIN	CARBS	SUGARS	SALT	FIBER
504kcal	16.2g	3.5g	30.5g	62.8g	19.2g	1.7g	4.6g

CRISPY GOLDEN CHICKEN

CRUNCHY BACON BREADCRUMBS, AVO & CHILI SAUCE

SERVES 2 | TOTAL 15 MINUTES

2 x 5¼-oz skinless boneless
   chicken breasts

1 lemon

2 tablespoons all-purpose flour

2 slices of smoked bacon

1 oz sourdough breadcrumbs

½ a ripe avocado

1 tablespoon plain yogurt

hot chili sauce, to serve

Lightly score the chicken breasts on one side, then place between two sheets of parchment paper and bash and flatten to ½ inch thick with a rolling pin, or the bottom of a pan. Rub all over with sea salt and black pepper, and half the lemon juice. Put the flour on a plate and gently turn the chicken in it to coat. Finely chop the bacon. Place a large non-stick frying pan on a medium-high heat with 1 tablespoon of olive oil, then add the chicken and bacon to get golden for 3 minutes. Turn the chicken, stir the breadcrumbs into the bacon and cook for 3 more minutes, or until the chicken is cooked through and the crumbs are golden.

At the same time, peel the avocado, scoop the flesh into a pestle and mortar, then smash up until smooth. Muddle in the yogurt and a squeeze of lemon juice, and season to perfection. Spoon over your plates or a platter, sit the chicken on top and sprinkle over the crunchy bacon breadcrumbs. Drizzle erratically with chili sauce, and serve with lemon wedges, for squeezing over.

ENERGY	FAT	SAT FAT	PROTEIN	CARBS	SUGARS	SALT	FIBER
414kcal	17.4g	3.9g	41.2g	23.7g	1.6g	1.2g	0.6g

CHICKEN NOODLE SOUP
GINGER, RENDANG SPICE, CRUNCHY VEG & COCONUT MILK

SERVES 4 | **TOTAL 20 MINUTES**

2 x 5¼-oz skinless boneless chicken breasts

3 tablespoons rendang curry paste

4-inch piece of fresh ginger

4 cups fresh chicken stock

1 x 14-oz can of light coconut milk

7 oz whole-wheat noodles

5½ oz baby corn

1 x 10-oz package of mixed stir-fry veg

Put a large non-stick frying pan and a large, deep pan on a medium heat. Slice each chicken breast into three long strips and massage with half the rendang paste and a pinch of sea salt and black pepper. Use a ball of paper towel to lightly rub the frying pan with olive oil, then add the chicken. Peel the ginger and chop into matchsticks. Sprinkle half over the chicken, then cook for 5 minutes, turning regularly and letting the chicken get dark and gnarly — you want it to almost blacken.

Alongside, sprinkle the rest of the ginger and rendang paste into the deep pan, pour in the stock and bring to a boil. Go in with the coconut milk and noodles, halve the corn lengthways and add to the pan, then cover and cook for 5 minutes. Stir in the mixed veg for a final minute until piping hot, then season to perfection and divide between warm bowls. Add 1 tablespoon of red wine vinegar to the chicken pan to deglaze it, moving the chicken around to pick up all those dark sticky bits. Cut the chicken pieces in half, and serve on top of your noodle soup.

ENERGY	FAT	SAT FAT	PROTEIN	CARBS	SUGARS	SALT	FIBER
456kcal	10.5g	6g	33.6g	55.3g	9.2g	1.5g	5.1g

1 SAUSAGE & MASH PIE

CREAMY LEEKS, MUSTARD, THYME & APPLE

2 MY FAVORITE SPEEDY SAUSAGE PIZZA

RED ONION, MOZZARELLA, FRAGRANT ROSEMARY, SWEET GRAPES & PINE NUTS

3 SAUSAGE CASSEROLE

HP SAUCE, MIXED BEANS & GIANT MASHED POTATO DUMPLING BALLS

4 SAUSAGE PASTA

DRIED CHILI, FENNEL, TOMATOES, BROCCOLINI & PARMESAN

5 SAUSAGE SILKY OMELET

AVOCADO, CHERRY TOMATOES, SOFT TORTILLAS & CHILI SAUCE

6 SAUSAGE CALZONE

STUFFED WITH CHEESE, ONION MARMALADE & AN EGG

7 ONE-PAN SAUSAGE HASH

BUTTERNUT SQUASH, POTATO, CARAWAY SEEDS & FRIED EGGS

SAUSAGES

SAUSAGE & MASH PIE

CREAMY LEEKS, MUSTARD, THYME & APPLE

SERVES 4 | TOTAL 1 HOUR 30 MINUTES

2½ lbs potatoes

6 Cumberland or other good-quality, herby pork or veggie sausages

2 large leeks

2 eating apples

½ a bunch of thyme (½ oz)

¼ cup all-purpose flour

2½ cups reduced-fat (2%) milk

3 teaspoons English mustard

Preheat the oven to 400°F. Peel the potatoes, chop into even-sized chunks and cook in a large pan of boiling salted water for 15 minutes, or until tender. Meanwhile, brown the sausages in a large non-stick casserole pan on a medium heat, tossing regularly (if using veggie sausages, add 1 tablespoon of olive oil), while you trim the leeks, halve lengthways, wash and slice ½ inch thick. Peel, core and chop the apples into ½-inch chunks. Once golden, remove the sausages to a plate, put the leek and apple into the pan and strip in most of the thyme. Add a splash of water, season with sea salt and black pepper, then cover and cook for 20 minutes, stirring occasionally. Drain the potatoes, mash with half the flour, then season to perfection. Lightly rub a 11- x 8-inch baking dish with oil.

Once the mash is cool enough to handle, use your fingertips to spread two-thirds of it evenly across the base and sides of the dish. Stir the remaining flour into the leeks, then gradually stir in the milk, then the mustard. Simmer for 5 minutes, or until thick and creamy. Slice the sausages ½ inch thick and stir most of them into the pan, along with any juices, then evenly spoon into the mash-lined dish. Press the remaining mash onto a sheet of parchment paper until just bigger than your dish, then flip over the top of the dish, peel off the paper, trim any excess and crimp the edges with a fork to seal. Poke the reserved sausage slices into the top, then gently brush with 1 tablespoon of oil. Bake at the bottom of the oven for 40 minutes, or until golden, adding the remaining thyme leaves for the last 5 minutes.

These values are based on cooking with Cumberland sausages.

ENERGY	FAT	SAT FAT	PROTEIN	CARBS	SUGARS	SALT	FIBER
647kcal	21.6g	8g	29.8g	88.2g	19g	2.4g	7.8g

MY FAVORITE SPEEDY SAUSAGE PIZZA
RED ONION, MOZZARELLA, FRAGRANT ROSEMARY, SWEET GRAPES & PINE NUTS

SERVES 2 | TOTAL 30 MINUTES

1 heaping cup self-rising flour, plus extra for dusting

2 Cumberland or other good-quality, herby pork or veggie sausages

1 small red onion

1 sprig of rosemary

1 heaping tablespoon sun-dried tomato paste

3½ oz red seedless grapes

1 x 4½-oz ball of mozzarella cheese

1 tablespoon pine nuts

Preheat the oven to full whack (475°F). Pile the flour into a bowl with a small pinch of sea salt, add ⅓ cup of water and mix into a dough, then knead on a flour-dusted surface for 2 minutes, adding a little extra flour, if needed. Roll and stretch out into a large oval (about 12 x 6 inches), then place in a large sturdy oiled pan. Cover with a clean damp kitchen towel and leave to rest while you put a small non-stick frying pan on a medium-high heat, then squeeze balls of sausagemeat out of the skins into the pan (if using veggie sausages, roughly slice and use 1 tablespoon of olive oil for frying). Fry until golden all over, tossing regularly, while you peel the red onion and slice super finely, ideally on a mandolin (use the guard!). Pick the rosemary leaves and toss with the onion, a pinch of sea salt and black pepper and 1 tablespoon of oil until well coated.

Spread the tomato paste over the dough, sprinkle over the dressed red onion and spoon over the sausage balls. Toss the grapes into the pan for 1 minute, then spoon over the pizza with any juices, tear over the mozzarella and sprinkle with the pine nuts. Place the pan over a high heat on the stove until it starts to sizzle, then cook at the bottom of the oven for 10 minutes, or until golden and crisp.

These values are based on cooking with Cumberland sausages.

ENERGY	FAT	SAT FAT	PROTEIN	CARBS	SUGARS	SALT	FIBER
826kcal	47.5g	15.7g	30.1g	73g	13.9g	2.7g	4.9g

SAUSAGE CASSEROLE

HP SAUCE, MIXED BEANS & GIANT MASHED POTATO DUMPLING BALLS

SERVES 4 | TOTAL 1 HOUR

6 Cumberland or other good-quality, herby pork or veggie sausages

1¾ lbs potatoes

2 heaping teaspoons grainy mustard

2 large carrots

2 leeks

3 tablespoons HP sauce

2 x 15-oz cans of mixed beans

1 x 14-oz can of plum tomatoes

Place the sausages in a large non-stick casserole pan on a medium-high heat with 1 tablespoon of olive oil and brown for 10 minutes, turning regularly, then remove to a plate, leaving the pan on the heat. Meanwhile, peel the potatoes, chop into even-sized chunks and cook in a large pan of boiling salted water for 15 minutes, or until tender, then drain and leave to steam dry. Mash well with half the mustard, then season to perfection. Trim, wash and chop the carrots and leeks into ¾-inch chunks. Stir into the fat in the pan and cook for 15 minutes, or until softened, stirring regularly, and adding a splash of water, if needed. Stir the HP sauce and remaining mustard into the veg, then pour in the beans, juice and all. Add the tomatoes, breaking them up with the spoon, then stir in 1 can's worth of water. Bring to a boil and cook for another 10 minutes, then season to perfection.

Preheat the broiler to high. Score the sausages at ¼-inch intervals and sit them cut-side up in the stew. As soon as the mash is cool enough to handle, divide it into four compact balls, push them into the stew and brush with 2 tablespoons of oil. Broil on the top rack of the oven for 15 minutes, or until golden and bubbling.

These values are based on cooking with Cumberland sausages.

ENERGY	FAT	SAT FAT	PROTEIN	CARBS	SUGARS	SALT	FIBER
673kcal	29.7g	7.7g	30.8g	68.8g	12.2g	1.8g	15.3g

SAUSAGE PASTA

DRIED CHILI, FENNEL, TOMATOES, BROCCOLINI & PARMESAN

SERVES 4 | TOTAL 35 MINUTES

8 chipolata or small pork sausages,
  or veggie sausages

2 red onions

1 tablespoon fennel seeds

1 teaspoon dried chili flakes

11 oz broccolini

2 x 14-oz cans of plum tomatoes

10 oz dried farfalle

¾ oz Parmesan cheese

Poach the sausages in a large pan of boiling salted water for 5 minutes (if using veggie sausages, there's no need to poach). Meanwhile, peel the onions, chop into ½-inch dice and place in a large shallow casserole pan on a medium heat with ½ a tablespoon of olive oil, the fennel seeds, chili flakes, a small pinch of sea salt and a good pinch of black pepper, stirring regularly. Scoop the sausages out onto a board, carefully finely slice, then stir into the onions. Trim the tough ends off the broccolini and finely slice the remaining stalks, leaving the tips whole. Add the stalks to the onions and cook for 10 minutes, or until softened, stirring regularly.

Tip the tomatoes into the onions and sausages, breaking them up with your spoon. Reduce to a simmer while you cook the pasta in the pan of boiling salted water according to the package instructions, adding the broccolini tips for just the last minute. Drain the pasta and broccolini, reserving a cupful of starchy cooking water. Toss through the sauce, loosening with a splash of reserved cooking water, if needed. Season to perfection, then finely grate over the Parmesan to finish.

These values are based on cooking with chipolata sausages.

ENERGY	FAT	SAT FAT	PROTEIN	CARBS	SUGARS	SALT	FIBER
306kcal	17.9g	5.8g	21g	17.1g	14.2g	1.2g	7.1g

SAUSAGE SILKY OMELET

AVOCADO, CHERRY TOMATOES, SOFT TORTILLAS & CHILI SAUCE

SERVES 2 | TOTAL 10 MINUTES

3 chipolata or small pork sausages, or veggie sausages

3½ oz ripe mixed-color cherry tomatoes

½ a ripe avocado

4 large eggs

¾ oz red Leicester cheese or other English Cheddar

2 whole-grain tortillas

1 tablespoon sour cream

hot chili sauce, to serve

Squeeze the sausagemeat out of the skins into a 12-inch non-stick frying pan on a medium-high heat (if using veggie sausages, finely chop and use 1 tablespoon of olive oil for frying). Break it up with a wooden spoon and fry until golden, stirring regularly, while you quarter the tomatoes, then scoop out the avocado and finely slice. Add the tomatoes to the pan for 2 minutes, stirring regularly, then remove half the contents of the pan to a plate. Beat 2 eggs, pour into the pan in one smooth action to cover the base, coarsely grate over half the cheese and cook for just a couple of minutes on the bottom only, so the egg is just set.

Slide the omelet onto a plate. Warm 1 tortilla in the pan for 30 seconds, then remove, halve and roll up. Spoon a bit of sour cream over the omelet, fan out half the avo on the side, and drizzle from a height with chili sauce. Let your lucky companion tuck in, while you quickly cook and serve the second portion.

These values are based on cooking with chipolata sausages.

ENERGY	FAT	SAT FAT	PROTEIN	CARBS	SUGARS	SALT	FIBER
579kcal	35.4g	11.9g	32.7g	30.9g	3.8g	1.8g	6.5g

SAUSAGE CALZONE

STUFFED WITH CHEESE, ONION MARMALADE & AN EGG

SERVES 2 | TOTAL 20 MINUTES

3 Cumberland or other good-quality, herby pork or veggie sausages

1 heaping cup self-rising flour, plus extra for dusting

1 oz Cheddar cheese

2 tablespoons onion marmalade

1 large egg

¾ oz watercress

tomato ketchup, to serve

English mustard, to serve

Squeeze the sausagemeat out of the skins into an 11-inch non-stick ovenproof frying pan on a medium-high heat, stirring regularly until golden, then turn the heat off (if using veggie sausages, roughly slice and use 1 tablespoon of olive oil for frying). Meanwhile, pile the flour into a bowl, add ⅓ cup of water and mix into a dough, then knead on a flour-dusted surface for 2 minutes, adding a little extra flour, if needed. Roll out into a circle about 12 inches across. Coarsely grate the cheese over one half, dollop over the marmalade and scatter over the sausage, returning the pan to a medium heat. Crack the egg on top of the other fillings, then fold over the dough into a semi-circle, pinching the edges to seal.

Gently place the calzone into the hot pan and cook for 5 minutes, or until golden and crisp, then carefully but confidently flip it over and cook for another 5 minutes on the other side. Slide it onto a board, let it stand for 2 minutes, then slice and serve with the watercress, with ketchup and mustard on the side for dunking.

These values are based on cooking with Cumberland sausages.

ENERGY	FAT	SAT FAT	PROTEIN	CARBS	SUGARS	SALT	FIBER
694kcal	34.1g	11.8g	29.9g	69.5g	10.2g	2.9g	3.1g

ONE-PAN SAUSAGE HASH

BUTTERNUT SQUASH, POTATO, CARAWAY SEEDS & FRIED EGGS

SERVES 2 | **TOTAL 35 MINUTES**

8 oz butternut squash

1 potato (8 oz)

1 red onion

3 Cumberland or other good-quality, herby pork or veggie sausages

2 teaspoons caraway seeds

¼ of a red cabbage (8 oz)

1 green eating apple

2 large eggs

Seed the squash, scrub with the potato and chop both into ½-inch dice. Peel the onion and chop the same size. Squeeze the sausagemeat out of the skins into a large non-stick frying pan on a medium-high heat (if using veggie sausages, roughly slice and use 1 tablespoon of olive oil for frying). Break it up with a wooden spoon and fry until lightly golden, stirring regularly. Sprinkle in most of the caraway seeds, then add the squash, potato and onion. Season with sea salt and black pepper, add 3 tablespoons of water, cover and cook for 20 minutes, or until golden and cooked through, stirring and smashing occasionally and scraping up any sticky bits.

Meanwhile, coarsely grate the red cabbage and toss in a little red wine vinegar, then coarsely grate the apple. Divide the hash between warm plates, leaving the pan on the heat. Put 1 tablespoon of oil into the pan, sprinkle in the remaining caraway seeds, crack in the eggs and fry to your liking, spooning over the oil and seeds as they cook. Quickly drain the eggs on paper towel, then place on top of the hash and serve sprinkled with the grated red cabbage and apple.

These values are based on cooking with Cumberland sausages.

ENERGY	FAT	SAT FAT	PROTEIN	CARBS	SUGARS	SALT	FIBER
650kcal	38.1g	9.7g	28.9g	53.2g	22.3g	1.9g	9.7g

1 CRISPY SALMON TACOS
CAJUN SPICE, MANGO, SWEET CHERRY TOMATOES & LIME

2 TERIYAKI CONCERTINA SALMON
GREEN TEA–INFUSED NOODLES, PICKLED GINGER & BROCCOLINI

3 CREAMY SHRIMP-STUFFED SALMON
WILTED GARLICKY SPINACH, SMOKY PANCETTA, ROSEMARY & PARMESAN

4 NEW-STYLE SALMON SASHIMI
LIME, CLEMENTINE & SOY DRESSING, SESAME SEEDS & CRISPY SALMON SKIN

5 EASY SALMON EN CROUTE
TASTY SPINACH, BAKED RED PESTO SAUCE & LEMON

6 CAJUN SALMON PO' BOY
JALAPEÑO SALSA, YOGURT, SHREDDED LETTUCE & TOMATO

7 CRISPY SWEET & SOUR SALMON
STIR-FRIED PUFFED RICE, MINT, SCALLIONS & LETTUCE CUPS

SALMON FILLET

CRISPY SALMON TACOS

CAJUN SPICE, MANGO, SWEET CHERRY TOMATOES & LIME

SERVES 2 | **TOTAL 20 MINUTES**

5 ½ oz ripe mixed-color cherry tomatoes

1 small ripe mango

½ a small ripe avocado

2 scallions

2 x 4 ½-oz salmon fillets, skin on, scaled, pin-boned

2 heaping teaspoons Cajun seasoning

4 small tortillas

2 limes

Quarter the cherry tomatoes. Pit, peel and roughly chop the mango. Scoop out the avocado and finely slice. Trim and finely slice the scallions. Carefully cut the skin off the salmon and place it in a non-stick frying pan on a medium-high heat to crisp up on both sides. Pat the Cajun seasoning all over the salmon fillets, then fry for 5 minutes, turning to get them golden on each of their sides. Once the skin is crispy, move it to sit on top of the salmon.

Meanwhile, use tongs to toast the tortillas directly over the flame of your gas stove for 15 seconds, or use a hot pan. Sprinkle the mango, avocado and scallions over the tortillas, then flake over the salmon and crack over the skin. Toss the tomatoes and the juice of 1 lime in the residual heat of the pan for 30 seconds, then spoon over the tortillas. Serve with lime wedges, for squeezing over.

ENERGY	FAT	SAT FAT	PROTEIN	CARBS	SUGARS	SALT	FIBER
584kcal	24.6g	5.8g	35g	59.5g	17g	1.8g	4.1g

TERIYAKI CONCERTINA SALMON

GREEN TEA-INFUSED NOODLES, PICKLED GINGER & BROCCOLINI

SERVES 2 | **TOTAL 15 MINUTES**

7 oz purple broccolini

2 x 4½-oz salmon fillets, skin on, scaled, pin-boned

1 green-tea bag

5¼ oz rice vermicelli noodles

2 scallions

1 tablespoon pickled ginger

2 tablespoons teriyaki sauce

You need a large steamer for this one. Boil the kettle. Trim the tough ends off the broccoli stalks. Place the salmon fillets skin-side down on a board and slice through the flesh at ¾-inch intervals, stopping just before you hit the skin. Pour ¾ inch of boiling kettle water into a large shallow pan on a high heat. Place an oiled steamer on top and sit the salmon fillets at either side, skin-side down, gently pushing each slice of salmon the opposite way to the next one, concertina-style, like in the picture. Pile the broccolini in the middle, put the lid on and steam for 5 minutes, or until just cooked. Meanwhile, in a heatproof bowl, cover the green-tea bag and noodles with boiling kettle water, stir gently and put aside. Trim and finely slice the scallions. Finely slice the pickled ginger.

Drain the noodles (discarding the tea bag). Divide the broccolini and salmon between your plates, then spoon the teriyaki sauce over the salmon with a little pickled ginger juice. Sprinkle over the scallions and ginger, then serve with the noodles.

ENERGY	FAT	SAT FAT	PROTEIN	CARBS	SUGARS	SALT	FIBER
583kcal	15.5g	2.7g	36g	74.2g	8g	1.4g	3.6g

CREAMY SHRIMP-STUFFED SALMON

WILTED GARLICKY SPINACH, SMOKY PANCETTA, ROSEMARY & PARMESAN

SERVES 4 | TOTAL 30 MINUTES

4 x 4½-oz salmon fillets, skin on, scaled, pin-boned

¾ oz Parmesan cheese

3 oz reduced-fat crème fraîche

3 oz small cooked peeled shrimp

4 cloves of garlic

1 lb spinach

4 slices of smoked pancetta or bacon

4 sprigs of rosemary

Preheat the oven to 425°F. Cut down the middle of each salmon fillet lengthways on the flesh side, going about three-quarters of the way through to make a pocket. Finely grate the Parmesan, beat with the crème fraîche, then mix in the shrimp.

Rub a large deep sturdy pan with a little olive oil and place on a low heat on the stove. Peel and finely slice the garlic, add to the pan with the spinach, season, stir until just wilted, then turn the heat off. Nestle in the salmon fillets, divide and spoon the shrimp mixture into the pockets, then sprinkle with black pepper. Drape one slice of pancetta over each fillet. Rub the rosemary sprigs with a little oil and place one on each piece of salmon. Cook in the oven for 15 minutes, then serve.

ENERGY	FAT	SAT FAT	PROTEIN	CARBS	SUGARS	SALT	FIBER
354kcal	21.3g	6g	36.7g	3.9g	2.6g	1g	0.2g

NEW-STYLE SALMON SASHIMI

LIME, CLEMENTINE & SOY DRESSING, SESAME SEEDS & CRISPY SALMON SKIN

SERVES 2 | TOTAL 15 MINUTES

3 tablespoons raw sesame seeds

2 x 4½-oz super-fresh chunky salmon
    fillets, skin on, scaled, pin-boned

1 lime

1 clementine

2 teaspoons reduced-sodium
    soy sauce

1 fresh red chili

1 cup sprouting cress

Toast the sesame seeds in a hot frying pan for 2 minutes, tossing until golden, then tip into a bowl and put aside. Return the pan to a medium heat. Cut each salmon fillet into four chunks, then carefully cut off the skin. Place the skin in the pan to crisp up on both sides, removing it when golden. Sear the salmon chunks for just 10 seconds on each side, turning with tongs. Remove from the pan and turn in the sesame seeds to coat on all sides, then slice ½ inch thick and arrange on your plates.

Finely grate some lime and clementine zest to sprinkle over at the end, then squeeze all the juice into a bowl and add the soy. Finely slice the chili. Snip the cress. Spoon the dressing over the salmon with a few drips of extra virgin olive oil, then sprinkle with the embellishments. Serve with the crispy salmon skin.

ENERGY	FAT	SAT FAT	PROTEIN	CARBS	SUGARS	SALT	FIBER
336kcal	23.1g	4.1g	29.7g	2.2g	2.2g	0.6g	0.2g

EASY SALMON EN CROUTE

TASTY SPINACH, BAKED RED PESTO SAUCE & LEMON

SERVES 4 | TOTAL 55 MINUTES

1 onion

4 cloves of garlic

1 lb frozen spinach

1 x 11-oz sheet of all-butter
puff pastry (cold)

4 x 4½-oz salmon fillets, skin off,
pin-boned

2 large eggs

1 heaping tablespoon red pesto

1 lemon

Preheat the oven to 425°F. Peel and chop the onion and place in a large non-stick pan on a medium heat with 1 tablespoon of olive oil. Peel, finely slice and add the garlic, then cook for 10 minutes, or until softened, stirring regularly. Stir in the spinach, cover, and cook for 5 minutes, then remove the lid and cook for another 5 minutes, or until all the liquid has cooked away. Season to perfection. Unroll the pastry and place it, still on its paper, in a baking pan. Spread over the spinach, leaving a 2-inch border all the way around. Sit the salmon fillets on top, ½ inch apart, then use the paper to help you fold in the pastry edges to snugly encase the salmon, leaving it exposed on the top. Beat the eggs and use some to brush the exposed pastry, then bake at the bottom of the oven for 15 minutes.

Meanwhile, beat the pesto into the remaining egg. When the time's up, pull out the pan and pour the egg mixture over the salmon and into the gaps. Return to the bottom of the oven for a final 15 minutes, or until the pastry is golden and the egg is just cooked through. Serve with lemon wedges, for squeezing over.

ENERGY	FAT	SAT FAT	PROTEIN	CARBS	SUGARS	SALT	FIBER
712kcal	46.4g	18g	37g	36g	6.9g	1.3g	2.7g

CAJUN SALMON PO' BOY
JALAPEÑO SALSA, YOGURT, SHREDDED LETTUCE & TOMATO

SERVES 2 | **TOTAL 20 MINUTES**

1 x 7½-oz jar of sliced green jalapeños

1 bunch of cilantro (1 oz)

2 heaping teaspoons Cajun seasoning

4 heaping tablespoons Greek yogurt

2 x 4½-oz salmon fillets, skin on, scaled, pin-boned

1 little gem lettuce

1 large ripe tomato

2 submarine rolls

Pour the jalapeños and their liquor into a blender, then rip in the top leafy half of the cilantro and blitz until smooth. Pour back into the jar and put aside. In a bowl, mix the Cajun seasoning with half the yogurt. Cut the salmon fillets in half lengthways, then toss in the spiced yogurt until well coated. Place a large non-stick frying pan on a medium-high heat. Once hot, cook the salmon in ½ a tablespoon of olive oil for 4 minutes, turning until golden and gnarly all over. Meanwhile, very finely shred the lettuce. Finely slice and season the tomato.

Halve and lightly toast the rolls. Spread half the remaining yogurt across the bases, sit the tomato on top, then the lettuce. Tear over the gnarly salmon pieces, then spoon over the rest of the yogurt and some jalapeño salsa (keep the rest of the jar in the fridge for future meals), pop the tops on and enjoy.

ENERGY	FAT	SAT FAT	PROTEIN	CARBS	SUGARS	SALT	FIBER
540kcal	23.6g	5.9g	36.4g	44.9g	9.8g	1.5g	4g

CRISPY SWEET & SOUR SALMON

STIR-FRIED PUFFED RICE, MINT, SCALLIONS & LETTUCE CUPS

SERVES 2 | TOTAL 15 MINUTES

2 x 4½-oz salmon fillets, skin on,
scaled, pin-boned

4 scallions

2 cloves of garlic

½ a bunch of mint (½ oz)

1 little gem lettuce

2 tablespoons chili jam or red pepper
jelly

½ a lemon

2 cups puffed brown rice

Place the salmon skin-side down in a large non-stick frying pan on a medium-high heat with ½ a tablespoon of olive oil. Let the skin get super crispy for 4 minutes, then turn the salmon, giving it 1 minute on each of the other sides. Use tongs to pull off the crispy skin and place it in the pan alongside, turning the salmon to crisp up the newly exposed side. Meanwhile, trim and slice the scallions. Peel and finely slice the garlic. Pick the mint leaves. Click the lettuce apart into cups.

Lift the salmon out onto warm plates, brush with half the chili jam and add a squeeze of lemon juice. Hang the crispy skin over the salmon so it bends, leaving the pan on the heat. Fry the garlic and mint leaves for 1 minute, then toss in the scallions, puffed rice and remaining chili jam. Toss for 2 more minutes, then season to perfection and serve with the salmon and lettuce cups, for scooping.

ENERGY	FAT	SAT FAT	PROTEIN	CARBS	SUGARS	SALT	FIBER
422kcal	18.3g	3.1g	29.9g	34.4g	13.9g	0.5g	1.7g

1 SWEET POTATO BURGER

BEEF PATTY, BBQ SAUCE, CHARRED SWEET POTATO, COTTAGE CHEESE & SLAW

2 SWEET POTATO & CHICKEN CHOP SUEY

LIME, SWEET CHILI & OYSTER SAUCES, BABY CORN, SCALLIONS & FLUFFY RICE

3 SWEET POTATO STEW

BEANS, BAY, SCOTCH BONNET CHILI, PITAS & FETA CHEESE

4 SIZZLING SWEET POTATO WEDGES

CHOPPED SALAD, SWEET PEPPER & SOUR CREAM DRESSING & FETA CHEESE

5 SWEET POTATO OPEN QUESADILLA

CRISPY BLACK BEANS, JERK SPICES, JALAPEÑOS & MELTED CHEESE

6 SWEET POTATO & SALMON POKE BOWL

JUICY PINEAPPLE, CUCUMBER, TOMATOES, FRESH CHILI, MINT & LEMON

7 SWEET POTATO CHOWDER

CHORIZO, SCALLIONS, GREEN BEANS, CREAM & CRACKERS

SWEET
POTATO

SWEET POTATO BURGER

BEEF PATTY, BBQ SAUCE, CHARRED SWEET POTATO, COTTAGE CHEESE & SLAW

SERVES 2 | TOTAL 15 MINUTES

1 sweet potato (8 oz)

1¾ oz green cabbage

1 heaping teaspoon grainy mustard

8 oz ground beef

2 tablespoons BBQ sauce

2 large soft buns

1 little gem lettuce

2 tablespoons cottage cheese

Scrub the sweet potato. Slice three-quarters of it into ¼-inch rounds and place in a large non-stick frying pan on a medium-high heat with 1 tablespoon of olive oil to soften and char, turning after a few minutes. Meanwhile, coarsely grate the remaining sweet potato and the cabbage. Mix with the mustard and 1 tablespoon of red wine vinegar to make a slaw, then season to perfection.

Scrunch up the ground beef, divide into two and shape into patties, then season with sea salt and black pepper. Fry alongside the sweet potato slices for 3 minutes on each side, or until cooked through, brushing with the BBQ sauce for the final minute. Halve and lightly toast your buns, then pile on the slaw and add a few lettuce leaves. Arrange the charred sweet potato slices on top, then add the burgers and cottage cheese. Squash your bun lids on top and tuck in.

ENERGY	FAT	SAT FAT	PROTEIN	CARBS	SUGARS	SALT	FIBER
615kcal	16.2g	4.6g	40g	81.2g	14.3g	2.9g	8.3g

SWEET POTATO & CHICKEN CHOP SUEY

LIME, SWEET CHILI & OYSTER SAUCES, BABY CORN, SCALLIONS & FLUFFY RICE

SERVES 2 | TOTAL 25 MINUTES

1 sweet potato (8 oz)

2 skinless boneless chicken thighs

½ cup basmati rice

2 limes

2 tablespoons oyster sauce

1 tablespoon sweet chili sauce

5½ oz baby corn

1 bunch of scallions

Scrub the sweet potato and chop into ½-inch-thick chips about 1½ inches in length. Place in a large dry non-stick frying pan on a medium-high heat to soften and char for 10 minutes, stirring regularly. Cut the chicken into similar-sized strips and add to the pan for another 5 minutes. Put ½ cup of rice, 1 cup of boiling kettle water and a small pinch of sea salt in a small pan. Cover, and cook on a medium heat for 12 minutes, or until all the water has been absorbed.

Meanwhile, finely grate the zest of 1 lime into a bowl, squeeze in the juice, then stir in the oyster and sweet chili sauces, along with 7 tablespoons of water. Halve the baby corn lengthways, then toss into the sauce. Trim the scallions, chop into 1¼-inch lengths and toss into the sweet potato pan to cook for 3 more minutes. Pour in the corn and sauce, let it sizzle and cook down for just 2 minutes, then season to perfection and serve with the rice and lime wedges, for squeezing over.

ENERGY	FAT	SAT FAT	PROTEIN	CARBS	SUGARS	SALT	FIBER
645kcal	9.3g	2.1g	31.7g	112.4g	16.9g	1.8g	5.9g

SWEET POTATO STEW

BEANS, BAY, SCOTCH BONNET CHILI, PITAS & FETA CHEESE

SERVES 2 | TOTAL 30 MINUTES

4 fresh bay leaves

1 fresh Scotch bonnet chili

4 cloves of garlic

2 sweet potatoes (8 oz each)

1 x 15-oz can of mixed beans

1 x 14-oz can of plum tomatoes

1 oz feta cheese

2 pita breads

Put a 12-inch non-stick frying pan on a medium-low heat with 1 tablespoon of olive oil and the bay. Prick and add the whole chili. Peel and add the whole garlic cloves. Scrub the sweet potatoes, slice them into ¾-inch-thick rounds and add to the pan to cook for 10 minutes, turning halfway. Pour in the beans (juice and all), and the tomatoes. Break up the tomatoes with a wooden spoon, then cover the pan and simmer for 10 minutes, or until the sweet potatoes are cooked through.

Remove the lid, turn the heat up and let it bubble away for a few more minutes, or until the sauce is nice and thick. Toast the pita bread. Season the stew to perfection, then crumble over the feta. Serve with toasted pita, for dunking.

ENERGY	FAT	SAT FAT	PROTEIN	CARBS	SUGARS	SALT	FIBER
652kcal	11.9g	3.3g	23.9g	111.6g	21.5g	1.4g	18.5g

SIZZLING SWEET POTATO WEDGES
CHOPPED SALAD, SWEET PEPPER & SOUR CREAM DRESSING & FETA CHEESE

SERVES 4 | **TOTAL 50 MINUTES**

3 sweet potatoes (8 oz each)

2 tablespoons Cajun seasoning,
   plus extra for sprinkling

1 x 16-oz jar of roasted red peppers

3 tablespoons sour cream

1 English cucumber

8 oz ripe mixed-color cherry
   tomatoes

1 iceberg lettuce

2 oz feta cheese

Preheat the oven to 375°F. Scrub the sweet potatoes, slice them ½ inch thick, then halve each slice to give you wedges – I like to use a crinkle-cut knife for this. Toss with the Cajun seasoning, 1 tablespoon of olive oil and a small pinch of sea salt. Arrange in a single layer in your largest roasting pan and roast for 40 minutes, or until golden and cooked through, shaking halfway.

About 10 minutes before the wedges are done, drain the peppers and blitz half in a blender with the sour cream until smooth. On your largest board, roughly chop the rest of the peppers with the cucumber, tomatoes and lettuce, mixing as you go. Toss with the dressing and season to perfection. Crumble over the feta, then serve with the sizzling sweet potato wedges and an extra sprinkling of Cajun seasoning.

ENERGY	FAT	SAT FAT	PROTEIN	CARBS	SUGARS	SALT	FIBER
329kcal	15.8g	4.9g	8.3g	38.8g	17.9g	1.2g	8.3g

SWEET POTATO OPEN QUESADILLA

CRISPY BLACK BEANS, JERK SPICES, JALAPEÑOS & MELTED CHEESE

SERVES 2 | TOTAL 20 MINUTES

2 sweet potatoes (8 oz each)

2 large whole-grain tortillas

1 x 15-oz can of black beans

1½ teaspoons jerk seasoning

14 jarred sliced green jalapeños

1½ oz Cheddar cheese

4 sprigs of mint

1 lime

Preheat the broiler to high. Scrub the sweet potatoes, prick with a fork and microwave on full whack (800W) for 6 minutes, or until soft throughout.

Now, it's easiest to cook these one at a time, but you can assemble them together. Push one tortilla into an 8-inch non-stick ovenproof frying pan, and place the other on a plate. Use a fork to break up and squash one sweet potato into each tortilla. Drain and spoon over the black beans, dust with the jerk seasoning, sprinkle over the jalapeño slices and break over the cheese. Pop the pan under the broiler for 5 minutes, or until golden and the cheese has melted. Serve sprinkled with mint leaves and a good squeeze of lime juice, season to perfection and tuck in together while you get the second one into the pan and under the grill.

ENERGY	FAT	SAT FAT	PROTEIN	CARBS	SUGARS	SALT	FIBER
581kcal	11.2g	5.8g	23.2g	88.9g	13.1g	1.7g	25g

SWEET POTATO & SALMON POKE BOWL

JUICY PINEAPPLE, CUCUMBER, TOMATOES, FRESH CHILI, MINT & LEMON

SERVES 2 | TOTAL 40 MINUTES

2 small sweet potatoes (5¼ oz each)

2 lemons

2 x 4½-oz super-fresh salmon fillets, skin off, pin-boned

½ an English cucumber

5½ oz ripe mixed-color cherry tomatoes

¼ of a ripe pineapple

½ a bunch of mint (½ oz)

1–2 fresh mixed-color chilies

Scrub the sweet potatoes, then cook them whole in a pan of boiling salted water for 35 minutes, or until beautifully soft throughout.

About 10 minutes before the sweet potatoes are ready, squeeze the lemon juice into two serving bowls. Add 1 tablespoon of extra virgin olive oil to each, and season with sea salt and black pepper. Chop the salmon into ½-inch chunks and divide between the bowls, tossing through the dressing to lightly cure it. Chop the cucumber, tomatoes and peeled pineapple into ½-inch chunks and add to the bowls. Roughly chop and add the mint leaves. Finely slice and add the chili (as much as you like), then toss everything in the dressing. Gently remove the skin from the sweet potatoes and add to the story. I love spooning off a little hot slice of soft sweet potato to pair with the cold dressed salad. Eat right away.

ENERGY	FAT	SAT FAT	PROTEIN	CARBS	SUGARS	SALT	FIBER
483kcal	21.5g	3.5g	30.7g	42.7g	18.3g	0.9g	6.7g

SWEET POTATO CHOWDER
CHORIZO, SCALLIONS, GREEN BEANS, CREAM & CRACKERS

SERVES 4 | TOTAL 40 MINUTES

3 oz chorizo

1 bunch of scallions

2 sweet potatoes (8 oz each)

14 oz mixed chopped onion,
    carrot & celery

7¾ oz green beans

⅓ cup heavy cream

3 oz plain crackers

Finely slice the chorizo, place in a large non-stick pan and put it on a medium heat to crisp up while you trim and finely slice the scallions, saving the green slices for garnish. Peel and dice the sweet potatoes so they're twice the size of those in your chopped veg bag. Once the chorizo is lightly golden, stir in all the chopped veg. Cook for 10 minutes on a low heat, or until softened, stirring occasionally. Pour in 4 cups of boiling kettle water and simmer for 10 minutes. Chop the green beans into ¾-inch lengths, then add to the pan to simmer for a final 10 minutes.

Stir in the cream, season to perfection and divide between four bowls. Sprinkle over the greens of the scallions, and finish with a few drips of extra virgin olive oil. Crush up all the crackers, adding sprinkles to the soup as you tuck in.

ENERGY	FAT	SAT FAT	PROTEIN	CARBS	SUGARS	SALT	FIBER
345kcal	13.8g	6.2g	11.2g	45.6g	11.4g	1.2g	7.7g

1 ROASTED EGGPLANT LAKSA

MASSAMAN, GINGER, NOODLES, COCONUT MILK & CRUSHED CASHEWS

2 EGGPLANT & RICOTTA PASTA

CHILI PESTO, CAPERS, OREGANO, SMOKED ALMONDS & PECORINO

3 THAI RED EGGPLANT CURRY

SEARED STEAK, CRUSHED PEANUTS, FLUFFY RICE, COCONUT & LIME

4 MOREISH EGGPLANT SALAD

FETA CHEESE, MINT, OLIVES, ALMONDS, LEMON & HONEY

5 EGGPLANT PARMESAN MILANESE

QUICK SWEET TOMATO, GARLIC & BASIL SAUCE WITH SPAGHETTI

6 FUN HARISSA EGGPLANT CAKE

SWEET PEPPERS, FLUFFY COUSCOUS, OLIVES, ARUGULA & LEMON

7 WARM EGGPLANT SUSHI PLATE

CHILI JAM & PONZU GLAZE, NORI, SESAME, WASABI PEAS & RADISHES

EGGPLANT

ROASTED EGGPLANT LAKSA

MASSAMAN, GINGER, NOODLES, COCONUT MILK & CRUSHED CASHEWS

SERVES 6 | TOTAL 50 MINUTES

6 large eggplants (14 oz each)

6 heaping teaspoons massaman
    curry paste

2 oz honey-roasted cashew nuts

6 scallions

2½-inch piece of fresh ginger

1 x 14-oz can of light coconut milk

4 cups veg or chicken stock

1 lb egg noodles

Preheat the oven to 350°F. Slice 3 eggplants into ¾-inch-thick rounds. In a small bowl, mix 1 tablespoon each of olive oil and red wine vinegar, 1 heaping teaspoon of massaman paste and a small pinch of sea salt and black pepper, then brush on both sides of the sliced eggplants. Arrange in a single layer in a large roasting pan and roast for 40 minutes. Meanwhile, blacken the remaining 3 eggplants in a deep non-stick frying pan on a high heat, turning until charred and tender, then remove, leaving the pan on the heat. While they blacken, crush the cashews in a pestle and mortar, then put aside. Trim the scallions, chop the white halves (reserving the greens) and place in the pestle and mortar with the remaining massaman paste. Peel, chop and add the ginger, then pound into a paste. Finely slice the green scallions lengthways and put into a bowl of cold water to curl up.

I halve the charred eggplants and scoop the insides into the hot pan with 1 table-spoon of oil, discarding the skins. Stir in the paste for 2 minutes, then pour in the coconut milk, stock and 1 tablespoon of red wine vinegar and bring to a boil. Alongside, cook the noodles according to the package instructions, then drain and divide between warm bowls. Season the soup to perfection and ladle over the noodles, then top with the roasted eggplant slices. Drain the curly scallions and toss in a little red wine vinegar, then scatter over with the crushed cashews.

ENERGY	FAT	SAT FAT	PROTEIN	CARBS	SUGARS	SALT	FIBER
540kcal	18.3g	5.3g	17.4g	83.7g	14.9g	1.7g	14.5g

EGGPLANT & RICOTTA PASTA

CHILI PESTO, CAPERS, OREGANO, SMOKED ALMONDS & PECORINO

SERVES 2 | TOTAL 20 MINUTES

1 large eggplant (14 oz)

2 heaping teaspoons baby capers

1 teaspoon dried oregano, ideally the
    flowering kind, plus extra to serve

½ oz smoked almonds

5¼ oz dried pasta shells

2 heaping teaspoons chili
    & garlic pesto

1¾ oz ricotta cheese

½ oz pecorino or Parmesan cheese

Chop the eggplant into ½-inch chunks and place in a large non-stick frying pan on a medium-high heat with 1 tablespoon of olive oil, the capers, oregano and 2 tablespoons of water, then cover and steam for 5 minutes.

Meanwhile, crush the almonds in a pestle and mortar. Cook the pasta in a pan of boiling salted water according to the package instructions, then drain, reserving a cupful of starchy cooking water. Uncover the frying pan and let the eggplant fry for 10 minutes, or until lightly golden, stirring regularly. Add the pesto and most of the ricotta, followed by the pasta. Finely grate in the pecorino, then toss well over the heat, loosening with a splash of reserved cooking water. Season to perfection, then plate up. Sprinkle over the crushed almonds and an extra pinch of oregano, then add the remaining ricotta, to finish.

ENERGY	FAT	SAT FAT	PROTEIN	CARBS	SUGARS	SALT	FIBER
510kcal	20.1g	5.1g	17.5g	70g	7.7g	1.1g	8.6g

THAI RED EGGPLANT CURRY

SEARED STEAK, CRUSHED PEANUTS, FLUFFY RICE, COCONUT & LIME

SERVES 4 | TOTAL 30 MINUTES

1 cup basmati rice

2 large eggplants (14 oz each)

2 x 7½-oz sirloin steaks

1 bunch of scallions

1¾ oz dry roasted peanuts

2 tablespoons Thai red curry paste

1 x 14-oz can of light coconut milk

1 lime

Put 1 cup of rice, 2 cups of boiling kettle water and a pinch of sea salt into a deep non-stick pan on a medium heat, cover and cook for 12 minutes. Chop each eggplant into four chunky rounds and place on top of the rice for the last 8 minutes, keeping it covered. Meanwhile, cut off the sinew, season the steaks with a small pinch of sea salt and a pinch of black pepper, then use tongs to stand them fat-side down in a large non-stick frying pan on a medium-high heat, turning them onto the flat sides once crisp and golden. Sear on each side, cooking to your liking — I like mine medium rare. Trim the scallions and slice ¾ inch thick, adding them to the pan to lightly char alongside. Crush the peanuts in a pestle and mortar.

Move the steaks and scallions to a plate to rest. Use tongs to add the eggplant slices to the frying pan, leaving the rice covered with the heat off. Turn and char for 5 minutes, then stir in the curry paste, followed by the coconut milk and ½ a can of water. Boil for 8 minutes, or until the sauce is slightly thickened. Fluff up the rice and divide between warm plates, then slice and add the steaks, along with the scallions and the eggplant. Pour any resting juices into the sauce and spoon over. Sprinkle with the nuts and serve with lime wedges, for squeezing over.

ENERGY	FAT	SAT FAT	PROTEIN	CARBS	SUGARS	SALT	FIBER
582kcal	18.9g	8.9g	38.2g	69.7g	8.9g	1.4g	9.3g

MOREISH EGGPLANT SALAD

FETA CHEESE, MINT, OLIVES, ALMONDS, LEMON & HONEY

SERVES 2 | TOTAL 55 MINUTES

2 eggplants (8 oz each)

1 bunch of mint (1 oz)

¾ oz skin-on almonds

1 lemon

1 tablespoon liquid honey

8 mixed-color olives

1½ oz feta cheese

3½ oz mixed salad greens

Preheat the oven to 350°F. Place the whole eggplants directly on the bars of the oven and roast for 50 minutes, or until beautifully soft, tender and juicy.

Pick the baby mint leaves and put aside. Pick the rest of the leaves into a pestle and mortar, then add the almonds and roughly crush and pound together. Finely grate in the lemon zest, squeeze in the juice and muddle in with the honey and 2 tablespoons of extra virgin olive oil. Squash and pit the olives, tear the flesh into the mix and crumble in the feta. Mix it all together, then season to perfection with black pepper. Divide the salad and baby mint leaves between your plates. Slice the soft eggplants down the middle and place on top, then smother with the incredible, moreish pesto-style dressing. I like to attack the whole thing, chopping, tossing and mixing everything together as I tuck in. Delicious hot or cold.

ENERGY	FAT	SAT FAT	PROTEIN	CARBS	SUGARS	SALT	FIBER
340kcal	24.1g	5.3g	9g	25.1g	15.7g	0.8g	9.3g

EGGPLANT PARMESAN MILANESE
QUICK SWEET TOMATO, GARLIC & BASIL SAUCE WITH SPAGHETTI

SERVES 2 | **TOTAL 30 MINUTES**

1 eggplant (8 oz)	5 ¼ oz dried spaghetti
2 large eggs	2 cloves of garlic
3 ½ oz rosemary focaccia	1 x 14-oz can of cherry tomatoes
¾ oz Parmesan cheese	½ a bunch of basil (½ oz)

Preheat the oven to 350°F. Cut the skin off either side of the eggplant, then cut yourself four ½-inch-thick slices lengthways (saving any offcuts for another day). Sprinkle the slices with sea salt, and spend a couple of minutes gently bashing and tenderizing them with a meat mallet or rolling pin. Beat the eggs in a shallow bowl. Blitz the focaccia into fine crumbs in a food processor and pour onto a plate. Dip the eggplant slices in the egg, let any excess drip off, then dip each side in the crumbs. Fry in a large non-stick frying pan on a medium-high heat with 1 tablespoon of olive oil for 6 minutes, or until golden, turning halfway. Transfer to an oiled baking sheet, finely grate over most of the Parmesan and pop into the oven.

Cook the spaghetti in a pan of boiling salted water according to the package instructions. Wipe out the frying pan, returning it to a medium-high heat with ½ a tablespoon of oil. Peel, finely slice and add the garlic. Fry until lightly golden, pour in the tomatoes, then swirl a splash of water around the tomato can and into the pan. Pick the baby basil leaves and put aside, tear the rest into the sauce, season to perfection, then leave to simmer on a low heat. Once cooked, use tongs to drag the spaghetti straight into the sauce, letting a little starchy cooking water go with it. Toss together, then divide between plates. Sit the eggplant on top, grate over the remaining Parmesan and finish with the baby basil leaves.

ENERGY	FAT	SAT FAT	PROTEIN	CARBS	SUGARS	SALT	FIBER
688kcal	24.8g	5.7g	28.6g	92.5g	12g	1.6g	9.3g

FUN HARISSA EGGPLANT CAKE

SWEET PEPPERS, FLUFFY COUSCOUS, OLIVES, ARUGULA & LEMON

SERVES 4 | **TOTAL 30 MINUTES, PLUS CHILLING**

1 cup couscous

2 eggplants (8 oz each)

½ x 16-oz jar of roasted red peppers

2 heaping teaspoons rose harissa

1 lemon

2 oz arugula

8 green olives

¼ cup plain yogurt

Place the couscous in a bowl, add a pinch of sea salt and black pepper, then just cover with boiling kettle water, and cover. Slice the eggplants into ½-inch-thick rounds and, in batches, char on both sides in a grill pan on a high heat, removing to a bowl once soft. Thickly slice the peppers lengthways, add to the bowl with half the liquor from the jar, half the harissa and 2 tablespoons of extra virgin olive oil. Finely grate in the lemon zest, squeeze in the juice, mix and season to perfection.

Scrunch up a large wet sheet of parchment paper, then use it to line an 8-inch mixing bowl. Alternate the eggplant slices and strips of pepper inside, overlapping them slightly to cover (reserving the bowl of juices). Fluff up the couscous, roughly chop and scatter in most of the arugula (popping the rest in the fridge for later), stir in half the juices, then spoon it all into the veg-lined bowl, folding in any overhanging pepper and eggplant. Fold in the parchment, sit a plate on top with something heavy to compress it and put in the fridge for at least 2 hours. Mix together the remaining harissa and juices for later. Squash and pit the olives.

Once set, turn out your eggplant cake onto a nice serving plate or board and remove the parchment. Dollop over the yogurt, drizzle with the harissa dressing, scatter with the olives and remaining arugula, then slice and serve.

ENERGY	FAT	SAT FAT	PROTEIN	CARBS	SUGARS	SALT	FIBER
270kcal	9.9g	1.8g	7.7g	40.3g	7g	0.8g	6.6g

WARM EGGPLANT SUSHI PLATE

CHILI JAM & PONZU GLAZE, NORI, SESAME, WASABI PEAS & RADISHES

SERVES 2 | TOTAL 30 MINUTES

1 cup sushi rice

¾ oz wasabi peas

2 tablespoons raw sesame seeds

2 eggplants (8 oz each)

1¾ oz radishes

2 heaping tablespoons chili jam or red pepper jelly

2 tablespoons ponzu or reduced-sodium soy sauce

2–4 nori sheets

Cook the sushi rice according to the package instructions. Toast the wasabi peas and sesame seeds in a large non-stick frying pan on a medium heat as the pan heats up, then remove to a pestle and mortar. Halve the eggplants lengthways, lightly score each half on both sides in a criss-cross fashion, place skin-side down in the hot pan, pour in ¾ inch of water, cover and boil on a high heat for 15 minutes.

Meanwhile, finely slice the radishes and, in a bowl, mix with a small pinch of sea salt and 1 tablespoon of red wine vinegar to quickly pickle. Remove the lid from the eggplants and let any excess water cook away, then add 1 tablespoon of olive oil so it starts to fry and crisp up for a few minutes. Add the chili jam and ponzu and gently jiggle the pan so the eggplants glaze, then turn the heat off. Divide the rice between your plates, spoon over the eggplants and glaze from the pan, then crush and scatter over the peas and sesame seeds, along with the drained radishes. Scrunch up the nori sheets and serve on the side.

ENERGY	FAT	SAT FAT	PROTEIN	CARBS	SUGARS	SALT	FIBER
507kcal	16.2g	3g	13.2g	74.8g	13.6g	1.8g	2.9g

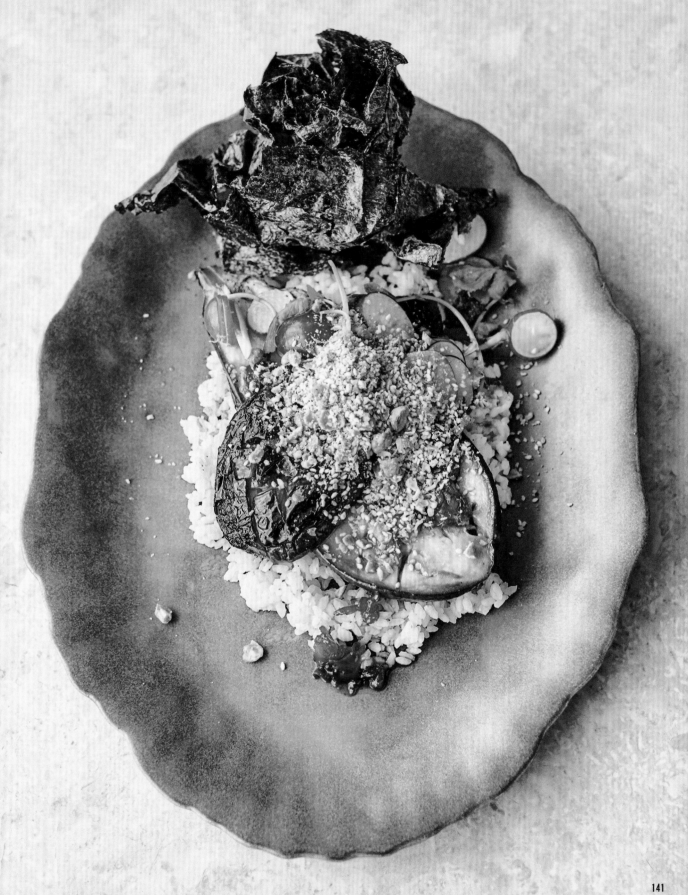

1 SPECIAL SCRAMBLED EGGS
QUICK STICKY SPICED TOMATO CHUTNEY STUFFED INTO SUPER-SOFT BUNS

2 HALLOUMI EGGY CRUMPETS
CHERRY TOMATO, LIME & AVOCADO SALSA & A RUNNY FRIED EGG

3 CAJUN CODDLED EGGS
HOME FRIES WITH SWEET POTATO, SWEET PEPPERS, CRISPY KALE & PANCETTA

4 ASIAN EGG & BEAN SALAD
SESAME, SOY, FRESH CHILI, LIME, SOY BEANS & SNOWPEAS

5 INDIAN-INSPIRED FRITTATA
TORN TOASTED CHAPATIS, BOMBAY MIX, CHEDDAR & CHUTNEY

6 EASY EGG & HAM PHYLLO BAKE
STUFFED WITH GRUYÈRE, APPLE, SPINACH & SCALLIONS

7 SUNSHINE EGG SALAD
DUKKAH & SWEET PEPPER GRAINS, WILTED SPINACH & POMEGRANATE

EGGS

SPECIAL SCRAMBLED EGGS
QUICK STICKY SPICED TOMATO CHUTNEY STUFFED INTO SUPER-SOFT BUNS

SERVES 2 | **TOTAL 20 MINUTES**

4 large eggs	1 teaspoon garam masala
2 soft buns	7 oz ripe tomatoes
1 red onion	½ a bunch of cilantro (½ oz)

Whisk and season the eggs. Halve the buns. Peel and coarsely grate the onion, then put 1 tablespoon into a bowl with a pinch of sea salt and a splash of red wine vinegar, and leave to quickly pickle. Scatter the rest into a large non-stick frying pan on a medium heat with 1 tablespoon of olive oil and most of the garam masala. Fry for 3 minutes, stirring often, while you coarsely grate the tomatoes. Push the onions aside and pour in the tomatoes to sizzle for 2 minutes. As soon as they start to dry out, mix and fry for 2 more minutes, or until thick, stirring occasionally.

Push the tomato chutney to one side, then toast the buns on both sides, wiping them around the pan to pick up any gnarly sticky bits. Spread the tomato chutney on the bun bases, tear off and pile on the cilantro leaves, squash the lids on top, then remove to your plates. Scramble the eggs to your liking and spoon alongside, then top with the drained pickled onion and serve dusted with garam masala.

ENERGY	FAT	SAT FAT	PROTEIN	CARBS	SUGARS	SALT	FIBER
415kcal	20.6g	4.5g	20.9g	40.4g	9.5g	1.7g	4.6g

HALLOUMI EGGY CRUMPETS

CHERRY TOMATO, LIME & AVOCADO SALSA & A RUNNY FRIED EGG

SERVES 1 | **TOTAL 10 MINUTES**

2 large eggs

2 crumpets

3 oz ripe mixed-color cherry
   tomatoes

1 teaspoon hot chili sauce

½ a lime

2 sprigs of cilantro

¼ of a small ripe avocado

¼ oz halloumi cheese

Beat one egg in a shallow bowl, then add the crumpets to soak on both sides. To make the salsa, quarter the tomatoes, then mix in a small bowl with the chili sauce and a squeeze of lime juice. Season to perfection, then pick over the cilantro leaves. Peel, chop and add the avocado, ready to toss just before serving.

Put a non-stick frying pan on a medium heat with 1 teaspoon of olive oil. Crack in the remaining egg, then add the crumpets alongside and cover. Flip the crumpets when golden, and cook the egg to your liking. Move it all to your plate, then quickly coarsely grate the halloumi into the pan. Toss the salsa and spoon over the crumpets. Once the halloumi is golden, use a slotted spatula to nudge it loose and flip it proudly over your plate, golden-side up. Finish with extra chili sauce, if you like.

ENERGY	FAT	SAT FAT	PROTEIN	CARBS	SUGARS	SALT	FIBER
450kcal	21.4g	5.7g	20.6g	43.7g	6.9g	1.8g	3.7g

CAJUN CODDLED EGGS
HOME FRIES WITH SWEET POTATO, SWEET PEPPERS, CRISPY KALE & PANCETTA

SERVES 4 | TOTAL 1 HOUR 20 MINUTES

2 red onions

2 mixed-color peppers

1 sweet potato (8 oz)

1 potato (8 oz)

2 heaping teaspoons Cajun seasoning

1¾ oz kale

4 slices of smoked pancetta or bacon

4 large eggs

Preheat the oven to 400°F. Peel the onions and cut into eighths. Halve and seed the peppers, scrub both potatoes, then chop them all into 1¼-inch chunks. Toss in a 14- x 10-inch roasting pan with the onions, Cajun seasoning and 1 tablespoon of olive oil. Roast at the bottom of the oven for 50 minutes. Meanwhile, tear up the kale, discarding any tough stalks, massage with 1 tablespoon of oil and put aside.

Get the pan out of the oven, poke the kale in and around the veg, drape over the pancetta and return to the oven for 5 minutes. Pull out the pan and crack in the eggs. Return to the oven for a final 5 minutes, or until the eggs are cooked to your liking. Season the eggs, then serve in the middle of the table.

ENERGY	FAT	SAT FAT	PROTEIN	CARBS	SUGARS	SALT	FIBER
309kcal	14.7g	3.2g	12g	34.3g	12.2g	0.7g	6.3g

ASIAN EGG & BEAN SALAD

SESAME, SOY, FRESH CHILI, LIME, SOY BEANS & SNOWPEAS

SERVES 2 | TOTAL 10 MINUTES

4 large eggs

5½ oz frozen soy beans

5½ oz snowpeas

1 fresh red chili

1 clove of garlic

2 limes

2 tablespoons tahini

1 tablespoon reduced-sodium
soy sauce

Cook the eggs in a pan of boiling salted water for 6 minutes, adding the soy beans and snowpeas to blanch for just the last 2 minutes, then drain it all.

Meanwhile, halve and seed the chili, peel the garlic, then pound both into a paste in a pestle and mortar. Finely grate the zest of 1 lime onto a board for later, then squeeze all the juice into the mortar and muddle in with the tahini. Stir in the soy to taste, using it to season the dressing. Toss the veg with 1 teaspoon of extra virgin olive oil and divide between your plates. Peel the eggs and sit them on top. Spoon over the dressing, burst the eggs and finish with a sprinkling of lime zest.

ENERGY	FAT	SAT FAT	PROTEIN	CARBS	SUGARS	SALT	FIBER
342kcal	22.5g	3.8g	23.7g	13.9g	4g	0.9g	4.7g

INDIAN-INSPIRED FRITTATA
TORN TOASTED CHAPATIS, BOMBAY MIX, CHEDDAR & CHUTNEY

SERVES 6 | TOTAL 25 MINUTES

4 whole-grain chapatis

8 large eggs

2 tablespoons mango chutney

1¾ oz mature Cheddar cheese

7 oz baby spinach

1 oz Bombay mix

½ a small red onion

2 tablespoons plain yogurt

Preheat the oven to 400°F. Put a 10-inch non-stick ovenproof frying pan on a medium heat and, one by one, lightly toast the chapatis. Meanwhile, in a large bowl, beat the eggs with half the mango chutney. Coarsely grate in most of the cheese, chop and add the spinach, then erratically tear in the toasted chapatis. Add a pinch of sea salt and black pepper and mix it all together well.

Put 1 tablespoon of olive oil into the frying pan, then pour in the egg mixture. Grate over the remaining cheese and sprinkle over the Bombay mix. Shake the pan over the heat for 1 minute, then transfer to the oven for 10 minutes, or until golden and set. Meanwhile, grate the onion, mix with a pinch of salt and 1 tablespoon of red wine vinegar and leave to quickly pickle. Serve the frittata dolloped with yogurt and the remaining mango chutney, sprinkled with the drained pickled red onion.

ENERGY	FAT	SAT FAT	PROTEIN	CARBS	SUGARS	SALT	FIBER
313kcal	16.3g	5.7g	17.2g	24.6g	5.2g	1.8g	2.9g

EASY EGG & HAM PHYLLO BAKE
STUFFED WITH GRUYÈRE, APPLE, SPINACH & SCALLIONS

SERVES 6 | TOTAL 1 HOUR

8 large eggs	7 oz baby spinach
2 eating apples	1 bunch of scallions
3 oz Gruyère cheese	5¼ oz cottage cheese
3½ oz quality sliced ham	6 sheets of phyllo pastry

Preheat the oven to 400°F. Beat the eggs in a large bowl. Coarsely grate in the apples and most of the Gruyère. Finely slice the ham. Roughly chop the spinach. Trim and finely slice the scallions. Add it all to the eggs with the cottage cheese and a pinch of black pepper, then beat together. Pour the mixture through a colander into another bowl, separating the eggs from the filling. Put the eggs aside.

Rub a deep 14- x 12-inch pan with olive oil. Lay out one sheet of phyllo, then evenly sprinkle over one-sixth of the filling. Roll up and place in the oiled pan, folding in the edges, if needed. Repeat with the remaining sheets of phyllo and the remaining filling. Brush the top with a little oil, then bake at the bottom of the oven for 20 minutes. Evenly pour over the reserved egg mixture, grate over the remaining cheese, then return to the oven for a final 10 minutes, or until golden.

ENERGY	FAT	SAT FAT	PROTEIN	CARBS	SUGARS	SALT	FIBER
354kcal	16.4g	6g	23.2g	31.2g	7.6g	1.5g	1.9g

SUNSHINE EGG SALAD

DUKKAH & SWEET PEPPER GRAINS, WILTED SPINACH & POMEGRANATE

SERVES 2 | TOTAL 15 MINUTES

2 tablespoons dukkah

1 x 8-oz package of mixed cooked grains

½ x 16-oz jar of roasted red peppers

7 oz baby spinach

4 large eggs

½ a pomegranate

2 heaping tablespoons plain yogurt

Put a large pan of salted water on to simmer for your eggs. Toast most of the dukkah in a large non-stick frying pan on a medium heat for 2 minutes, then tip in the grains. Drain, finely chop and add the peppers. Cook and stir for 5 minutes, season to perfection, then divide between your plates. Return the pan to the heat and quickly wilt the spinach. Season to perfection and divide over the grains.

Meanwhile, crack each egg into the simmering water in one fluid movement and poach for 3 minutes, or until cooked to your liking. Squeeze a little pomegranate juice into a bowl and ripple through the yogurt, then bash the pomegranate half with the back of a spoon so the remaining seeds tumble out. Drain the eggs on paper towel, then place on top of the spinach. Spoon over the pomegranate yogurt, then sprinkle with the remaining dukkah and the pomegranate seeds.

ENERGY	FAT	SAT FAT	PROTEIN	CARBS	SUGARS	SALT	FIBER
436kcal	18.9g	4.5g	23.5g	40.2g	8.4g	0.5g	8.3g

1 BEEF & GUINNESS HOTPOT
CARROTS, SAGE, ONION & SLICED POTATO TOPPING

2 GINGERY GARLICKY BLACK BEAN BEEF
FLUFFY RICE, EASY SILKEN OMELETS WITH FRESH CHILI & SCALLIONS

3 BACON RAREBIT BURGER
MUSHROOMS, GHERKIN & SOUR CREAM IN A SOFT BUN

4 A VERY BRITISH BOLOGNESE
ROSEMARY, PALE ALE, MUSHROOMS, CHEDDAR & SPECIAL PASTA

5 CRISPY LAMB KEBAB FLATBREAD
GARLIC, FRESH CHILI, CUMIN, MIXED GARDEN SALAD & FETA CHEESE

6 PORK & APPLE MEATBALLS
MUSTARD, MASHED POTATO, SOUR CREAM & CHIVE SAUCE

7 MY MEXICAN MEATLOAF
BLACK BEANS, SWEET RED PEPPERS & JALAPEÑOS

GROUND MEAT

BEEF & GUINNESS HOTPOT
CARROTS, SAGE, ONION & SLICED POTATO TOPPING

SERVES 4 | TOTAL 1 HOUR 30 MINUTES

4 carrots	1 heaping tablespoon blackcurrant jam
5¾ oz jarred pickled cocktail onions	1¾ lbs potatoes
1 lb lean ground beef (meat or veggie)	1 cup Guinness
1 bunch of sage (¾ oz)	4 cups veg or chicken stock

Preheat the oven to 350°F. Wash the carrots, cut into 1¼-inch chunks and place in a large shallow non-stick casserole pan on a high heat with 1 tablespoon of olive oil. Fry for 5 minutes, or until golden, stirring regularly. Drain and add the pickled onions, then add the ground beef in chunks. Cook for 15 minutes, stirring regularly. Halfway through, tear in the sage leaves, then add a pinch of sea salt and black pepper, and the jam, letting everything get dark, sticky and caramelized.

Meanwhile, scrub the potatoes. Chop 7 oz of potato, place in a blender and blitz with the Guinness until smooth. Pour the mixture into the pan, letting it cook away and thicken, then add the stock. Bring to a boil while you cut the remaining potatoes into slices just under ¼ inch thick. Once boiling, turn the heat off and gently arrange the potatoes on the surface of the stew, so it's completely covered. Drizzle with 1 tablespoon of oil and carefully transfer to the oven to cook for 1 hour, or until the potatoes are golden, crisp and cooked through.

These values are based on cooking with lean ground beef.

ENERGY	FAT	SAT FAT	PROTEIN	CARBS	SUGARS	SALT	FIBER
503kcal	13.8g	3.8g	38g	56g	16.4g	1.8g	6.2g

GINGERY GARLICKY BLACK BEAN BEEF

FLUFFY RICE, EASY SILKEN OMELETS WITH FRESH CHILI & SCALLIONS

SERVES 4 | TOTAL 40 MINUTES

1 lb lean ground beef (meat or veggie)	7 oz black bean sauce
2½-inch piece of fresh ginger	1 cup basmati rice
4 cloves of garlic	1 bunch of scallions
2 fresh red chilies	4 large eggs

Put the ground beef into a 10-inch non-stick frying pan on a high heat with 1 tablespoon of olive oil and plenty of black pepper, breaking it up with a spoon. Brown for 10 minutes, or until starting to caramelize, while you peel the ginger and garlic, and finely chop with 1 seeded chili. Stir that into the pan, pour in the black bean sauce and crush it all with a potato masher. Reduce to a medium heat and cook for another 10 minutes, mashing occasionally, until the mixture is dark and gnarly.

Meanwhile, put 1 cup of rice, 2 cups of boiling kettle water and a small pinch of sea salt into a medium pan. Cover and cook on a medium heat for 12 minutes, or until all the water has been absorbed. Trim the scallions, slice the white halves ½-inch thick and finely slice the green tops with the remaining chili. Stir the whites into the ground beef with 1 tablespoon of red wine vinegar. Let it sizzle, then pour in 1⅔ cups of boiling kettle water. Simmer for 5 minutes, or until nicely reduced into a lovely sea of ground beef, then divide between your plates with the rice.

Quickly wipe out the frying pan, return it to a high heat, then wipe an oiled ball of paper towel around it. Quickly beat and add 1 egg, swirling it around, then sprinkle with a quarter of the chili and scallion mixture. Cook for just 30 seconds, then use the back of a spoon to pull it in at the sides. Turn it out onto your first portion and repeat the process, until you've used up all the ingredients.

These values are based on cooking with lean ground beef.

ENERGY	FAT	SAT FAT	PROTEIN	CARBS	SUGARS	SALT	FIBER
534kcal	16.3g	5g	40.3g	60.7g	5.2g	1.6g	1.1g

BACON RAREBIT BURGER

MUSHROOMS, GHERKIN & SOUR CREAM IN A SOFT BUN

SERVES 1 | TOTAL 12 MINUTES

3 chestnut or cremini mushrooms

4½ oz ground beef

2 slices of smoked bacon

1 soft bun

2 heaping teaspoons sour cream

1 gherkin

1 oz Cheddar cheese

1 tablespoon Worcestershire sauce

Trim the stalk and base off each mushroom, giving you a beautiful cross section (saving the offcuts for another day). Place the mushrooms cut-side down on one side of a large dry non-stick frying pan on a high heat. Cook for 5 minutes while you scrunch and work the ground beef with your hands. Divide into two equal balls, flatten to just under ¼ inch thick, then push a slice of bacon onto each one.

Turn the mushrooms, put the burgers into the pan, bacon-side down, sprinkle with a pinch of sea salt and black pepper, and fry hard and fast for 2 minutes, pressing down with a slotted spatula to crisp up the bacon, then flip to fry for just 1 minute on the other side. Move the mushrooms on top of the burgers, then halve the bun and quickly toast alongside. Remove the bun to a serving board, spread with the sour cream, stack in your burgers and mushrooms, then slice and add the gherkin.

Off the heat, coarsely grate the cheese in a pile at the cleanest side of the pan, pour the Worcestershire sauce on top, then tilt the pan and stir vigorously for 30 seconds until it combines into an oozy consistency. Pour the rarebit mixture over the burger stack and put the bun lid on. Devour.

ENERGY	FAT	SAT FAT	PROTEIN	CARBS	SUGARS	SALT	FIBER
517kcal	24.3g	12.3g	42.3g	34.1g	4.6g	2.8g	2.3g

A VERY BRITISH BOLOGNESE

ROSEMARY, PALE ALE, MUSHROOMS, CHEDDAR & SPECIAL PASTA

SERVES 2 + 6 BOLOGNESE FREEZER PORTIONS | TOTAL 1 HOUR 30 MINUTES

2 sprigs of rosemary

14 oz chopped mixed onion, carrot & celery

8 oz chestnut or cremini mushrooms

1 lb lean ground meat (beef, pork or veggie)

2 cups pale ale

2 x 14-oz cans of plum tomatoes

8 oz fresh lasagne sheets

¾ oz Cheddar cheese

Put a large, shallow non-stick casserole pan on a medium-high heat. Pick and finely chop the rosemary leaves, then sprinkle into the pan with 1 tablespoon of olive oil to crisp up. Add the chopped mixed veg and cook for 10 minutes, stirring regularly, while you trim and finely chop the mushrooms. Stir them into the pan with the ground meat, breaking it up with your spoon. Cook for 15 minutes, or until golden and caramelized. Pour in the ale, let it cook away, then stir in the tomatoes and 1 can's worth of water, mashing it all with a potato masher. Simmer on a medium-low heat for 1 hour, mashing occasionally to thicken the texture. Season to perfection.

For 2 portions, either cut the lasagne sheets into ¾-inch slices or, for a bit of fun, stack up your sheets and cut ¾-inch slits into them at ¼-inch intervals all over. Cook in a large pan of boiling salted water for just 3 minutes, then scoop out and toss with 2 portions of Bolognese, loosening with a splash of pasta cooking water, if needed. Grate over the cheese, and serve right away. Batch up your leftover portions, cool and pop into the fridge or freezer for another day. Happiness.

These values are based on cooking with lean ground beef.

ENERGY	FAT	SAT FAT	PROTEIN	CARBS	SUGARS	SALT	FIBER
397kcal	10.5g	5.9g	25.6g	47.5g	7.4g	0.7g	2g

CRISPY LAMB KEBAB FLATBREAD

GARLIC, FRESH CHILI, CUMIN, MIXED GARDEN SALAD & FETA CHEESE

SERVES 2 | TOTAL 25 MINUTES

1¾ cups self-rising flour,
   plus extra for dusting

1 red onion

8.5 oz ground meat (lamb or veggie)

4 cloves of garlic

1 teaspoon cumin seeds

1 fresh red chili

1 oz feta cheese

1¾ oz mixed salad leaves

Pile the flour into a bowl, add ½ cup of water and mix into a dough. Knead on a flour-dusted surface for 2 minutes, then cover and leave to rest. Peel and finely chop the onion, then, in a little bowl, mix one-third of it with a pinch of sea salt and 1 tablespoon of red wine vinegar and leave to quickly pickle. Scrunch the ground meat into a 12-inch non-stick frying pan on a medium heat with ½ a tablespoon of olive oil and cook for 3 minutes, stirring and breaking it up with a spoon. Add the rest of the onion, then peel and finely grate in the garlic, add the cumin, and season lightly with salt and add a good pinch of black pepper. Stir well and cook for 3 more minutes, or until getting lightly golden. Meanwhile, roll and stretch the dough out into a 14-inch round.

Roughly chop the chili and stir into the ground meat with 1 tablespoon of red wine vinegar. Moving swiftly, lift the dough into the pan to cover the mixture, using a wooden spoon to push it right into the edges. Cover and cook for 5 minutes, or until puffed up and cooked through. Using oven gloves, pop a board over the pan and confidently but carefully turn out the flatbread. Crumble over the feta, sprinkle over the salad leaves, the pickled red onion and any juices, then roll, slice and enjoy.

These values are based on cooking with ground lamb.

ENERGY	FAT	SAT FAT	PROTEIN	CARBS	SUGARS	SALT	FIBER
726kcal	24.7g	10.5g	38.5g	94g	7.5g	2.4g	6g

PORK & APPLE MEATBALLS
MUSTARD, MASHED POTATO, SOUR CREAM & CHIVE SAUCE

SERVES 4 | **TOTAL 35 MINUTES**

1¾ lbs potatoes

1 lb lean ground pork

1 teaspoon grainy mustard

1 eating apple

5¼ oz soft white bread

4 cups fresh chicken stock

¼ cup sour cream

1 bunch of chives (¾ oz)

Peel the potatoes, chop into even-sized chunks and cook in a large pan of boiling salted water for 15 minutes, or until tender. Meanwhile, place the ground pork in a bowl with the mustard. Coarsely grate in the apple. Tear 2¾ oz of the bread crust into a blender and blitz into crumbs, then add to the bowl, season with sea salt and black pepper, and scrunch together well. With wet hands, divide into four, then divide each piece into eight, and roll into 32 balls in total. Bring the stock to a simmer in a large pan, then drop in the balls to poach for 5 minutes, or until cooked through.

Drain the potatoes, return to the pan, mash well with 1 tablespoon of extra virgin olive oil, then season to perfection. Divide between warm bowls, then use a slotted spoon to scoop out the balls, sitting them on top. Tear the soft inner part of the bread into the blender, with the sour cream and most of the chives. Pour in 1¼ cups of the stock and blitz until silky smooth and aerated. Season to perfection, then divide between the bowls. Finely chop and scatter over the remaining chives and drizzle with 1 tablespoon of extra virgin olive oil, to finish.

ENERGY	FAT	SAT FAT	PROTEIN	CARBS	SUGARS	SALT	FIBER
475kcal	16g	4.9g	32.1g	51.9g	5.5g	1.2g	4.3g

MY MEXICAN MEATLOAF

BLACK BEANS, SWEET RED PEPPERS & JALAPEÑOS

SERVES 4 | TOTAL 1 HOUR

1 red onion	1 x 15-oz can of black beans
2 red peppers	1 lb lean ground beef
14 jarred sliced green jalapeños	1 x 14-oz can of plum tomatoes
½ a bunch of cilantro (½ oz)	¼ cup sour cream

Preheat the oven to 425°F. Peel the onion, cut into wedges, then pull apart into petals. Halve and seed the peppers, chop into 1¼-inch chunks, then toss both with 1 tablespoon of olive oil in a 14- x 10-inch baking pan. Roast for 15 minutes, while you finely slice the jalapeño and the cilantro stalks, reserving the leaves. Drain the beans and put half into a large bowl with the ground beef, jalapeños and cilantro stalks. Add a good pinch of sea salt and black pepper, use your hands to scrunch it all together well, then shape into a loaf. Nestle the meatloaf in the middle of the onions and peppers in the pan. Roast for 15 minutes.

Remove the pan from the oven, drizzle 1 tablespoon of red wine vinegar around the meatloaf, scatter in the remaining beans and scrunch in the plum tomatoes, then swirl a small splash of water around the tomato can and into the pan. Stir the sauce together around the meatloaf, season and return to the oven for a final 15 minutes, or until the meatloaf is beautifully golden and cooked through. Serve dolloped with the sour cream and sprinkled with the cilantro leaves.

ENERGY	FAT	SAT FAT	PROTEIN	CARBS	SUGARS	SALT	FIBER
327kcal	12.9g	5.1g	33.2g	17.2g	10.7g	1.7g	9.7g

1 ESSEX HASSELBACK HOTPOT
TENDER LAMB, CARROTS, CIDER, SAGE & BRANSTON PICKLE

2 BOMBAY JACKET SPUDS
CARROT RAITA, GRATED CHILI & CRISPY MINT-SPIKED FRIED EGGS

3 CRISPY POTATO PIE
FILLED WITH CHEDDAR, RED LEICESTER, SCALLIONS & TOMATO

4 QUICK STUFFED POTATO NAANS
SPINACH, SWEET ONION, SPICE & MANGO CHUTNEY YOGURT

5 CRISPY POTATO-TOPPED FISH
ALMOND, BASIL & SUN-DRIED TOMATO PESTO & GREEN BEANS

6 POTATO LASAGNE
CREAMY ASPARAGUS SAUCE, GORGONZOLA & PESTO

7 MY RUSSIAN POTATO SALAD
BABY CORNICHONS, APPLES, CARROTS, PEAS & CHIVES

POTATO

ESSEX HASSELBACK HOTPOT

TENDER LAMB, CARROTS, CIDER, SAGE & BRANSTON PICKLE

SERVES 4 | TOTAL 2 HOURS

1 lb cubed stewing lamb	1 tablespoon Branston pickle
2 onions	2 tablespoons all-purpose flour
2 carrots	2 cups dry cider
1 bunch of sage (¾ oz)	1½ lbs new potatoes

Toss the lamb with sea salt and plenty of black pepper. Place in a shallow casserole pan on a high heat with 1 tablespoon of olive oil, turning until brown all over. Meanwhile, peel the onions and carrots and chop into chunks the same size as the lamb. Remove the lamb to a plate, leaving the fat behind in the pan. Reduce to a medium heat, stir in the onions and carrots, tear in the sage leaves and add a splash of water. Cook for 10 minutes, stirring occasionally. Put the lamb back in and stir in the pickle, then the flour. Pour in the cider and 2½ cups of water to cover.

Preheat the oven to 350°F. Place one potato on a board between the handles of two wooden spoons, and carefully slice at just under ¼-inch intervals all the way along (the spoons will stop you going all the way through). Repeat with the rest of the potatoes. Stir the stew, season to perfection, then push in the potatoes, cut-side up. Cook in the oven for 1 hour 30 minutes, or until the potatoes are golden and have sucked up loads of that lovely flavor.

ENERGY	FAT	SAT FAT	PROTEIN	CARBS	SUGARS	SALT	FIBER
591kcal	20.4g	8.2g	34.8g	63g	15g	1.1g	6g

BOMBAY JACKET SPUDS

CARROT RAITA, GRATED CHILI & CRISPY MINT-SPIKED FRIED EGGS

SERVES 2 | TOTAL 1 HOUR 10 MINUTES

2 baking potatoes

2 teaspoons garam masala,
    plus extra for sprinkling

2 large carrots

3 heaping tablespoons Greek yogurt

½ a bunch of mint (½ oz)

2 large eggs

1 fresh or frozen red chili

Preheat the oven to 400°F. Scrub the potatoes, stab them all over with a fork, then rub them with 1 teaspoon of olive oil, the garam masala and a pinch of sea salt. Place on a rimmed baking sheet and roast for 1 hour. Meanwhile, wash and finely grate the carrots, wrap in a clean kitchen towel and squeeze the kitchen towel well to remove any excess liquid. Tip into a bowl, mix with the yogurt and season to perfection.

Just before your potatoes are done, put a large non-stick frying pan on a medium-high heat with 1 tablespoon of oil. Pick in the mint leaves, and, after 1 minute, crack in the eggs. Sprinkle with a little extra garam masala and fry the eggs to your liking. Slice open the spuds and pile in the carrot raita. Finely chop the fresh chili and scatter over to taste, or finely grate over the frozen chili. Plate up the eggs alongside.

ENERGY	FAT	SAT FAT	PROTEIN	CARBS	SUGARS	SALT	FIBER
444kcal	17.7g	6.2g	16.9g	58.3g	10.9g	1.1g	6.1g

CRISPY POTATO PIE

FILLED WITH CHEDDAR, RED LEICESTER, SCALLIONS & TOMATO

SERVES 4 | **TOTAL 1 HOUR 30 MINUTES**

2 lbs potatoes

12 oz ripe tomatoes

1 bunch of scallions

1¾ oz Cheddar cheese

1¾ oz red Leicester cheese or other English Cheddar

1 lemon

2½ oz arugula

Peel the potatoes, chop into even-sized chunks and cook in a large pan of boiling salted water for 15 minutes, or until tender. Meanwhile, halve the tomatoes, squeeze out the seeds and dice the flesh. Toss with a good pinch of sea salt and sit the tomatoes in a sieve to drain. Trim and finely slice the scallions. Coarsely grate the cheeses. Squeeze out any excess water from the tomatoes and mix with the scallions and cheese. Lay out a 16- x 12-inch sheet of parchment paper.

Preheat the oven to 400°F. Drain the potatoes, then mash really well with 2 tablespoons of extra virgin olive oil and season to perfection. Tip the mash onto the sheet of parchment. Once cool enough to handle, flatten out with oiled hands to a rectangle about ½ inch thick. Spread the tomato mixture over one half, leaving a ¾-inch gap around the edge, then in one swift move use the paper to help you flip the other half of the mash on top. Unpeel the top half of parchment, then use the paper to help you slide the whole thing into a 12- x 8-inch baking pan. Rip off the overhanging half of the paper, then fold and press in the edges of the mash and patch up any gaps, using a knife to help you smooth it out and make a pattern, if you like. Brush with 1 tablespoon of olive oil and bake for 50 minutes, or until golden and crisp. Slice and serve with lemon-dressed arugula.

ENERGY	FAT	SAT FAT	PROTEIN	CARBS	SUGARS	SALT	FIBER
402kcal	19.3g	6.9g	13.1g	46.9g	5.1g	1.1g	4.8g

QUICK STUFFED POTATO NAANS

SPINACH, SWEET ONION, SPICE & MANGO CHUTNEY YOGURT

SERVES 4 | TOTAL 50 MINUTES

2¼ cups self-rising flour,
    plus extra for dusting

1 potato (8 oz)

2 onions

10 oz frozen spinach

1 heaping tablespoon Madras
    curry paste

2 heaping teaspoons mango chutney

2 heaping tablespoons plain yogurt

1½ oz feta cheese

Pile the flour into a large bowl, add ⅔ cup of water and mix into a dough, kneading for 3 minutes. Leave to rest. For the filling, peel the potato and onions, chop into 1¼-inch chunks and cook in a pan of boiling salted water for 10 minutes, then drain. Meanwhile, put the spinach and curry paste into a large non-stick pan on a low heat, cover, and leave to defrost and gently fry. Stir in the drained potatoes and onions. Cook on a medium-high heat until golden and a bit gnarly, mashing it up as you go, then spread across a plate to cool.

Divide your dough into two, shape into balls, then stretch and flatten into 6-inch rounds on a flour-dusted surface. Divide the cooled filling into two, shape into compact balls, sit one on each piece of dough, then gently pull the dough around the filling to seal. Pat and flatten the dough, pushing it back out to 6 inches. Cook each naan in the pan on a medium-low heat with 1 tablespoon of olive oil for 10 minutes, or until dark golden and puffed up, turning a few times. Ripple the mango chutney through the yogurt, and sprinkle the naans with feta. Slice up, and get dunking!

ENERGY	FAT	SAT FAT	PROTEIN	CARBS	SUGARS	SALT	FIBER
457kcal	9.9g	2.6g	14.1g	82.5g	13.5g	1.8g	4.5g

CRISPY POTATO-TOPPED FISH

ALMOND, BASIL & SUN-DRIED TOMATO PESTO & GREEN BEANS

SERVES 2 | TOTAL 20 MINUTES

1 potato (8 oz)

2 x 5-oz white fish fillets, skin off, pin-boned

5½ oz fine green beans

½ a bunch of basil (½ oz)

½ a clove of garlic

¾ oz blanched almonds

2 sun-dried tomatoes

¾ oz Parmesan cheese

Preheat the grill to high. Scrub the potato, then use a vegetable peeler to peel it into ribbons. In a bowl, toss the ribbons with the fish, 1 teaspoon of olive oil and a pinch of sea salt and black pepper. Place the fish in a non-stick baking pan, then take a bit of pride in arranging one layer of potato ribbons in waves on top of each fillet. Grill for 10 minutes, or until golden and cooked through (keep an eye on it).

Meanwhile, trim the green beans and cook in a pan of boiling salted water for 7 minutes, or until tender. Tear the top leafy half of the basil into a pestle and mortar, and pound into a paste with a pinch of salt. Peel and bash in the garlic, then pound in the almonds and 1 sun-dried tomato. Finely grate in most of the Parmesan, muddle in 3 tablespoons of extra virgin olive oil to loosen, then season to perfection. Finely chop the other sun-dried tomato. Serve the potato-topped fish with the green beans and pesto. Sprinkle with the chopped tomato, drizzle with a little extra virgin olive oil and finely grate over the rest of the cheese, to finish.

ENERGY	FAT	SAT FAT	PROTEIN	CARBS	SUGARS	SALT	FIBER
553kcal	34.9g	6g	35.4g	25.9g	3.2g	1.6g	4.3g

POTATO LASAGNE
CREAMY ASPARAGUS SAUCE, GORGONZOLA & PESTO

SERVES 6 | TOTAL 2 HOURS 10 MINUTES

2 bunches of asparagus (1 ½ lbs total)

2 onions

⅓ cup all-purpose flour

4 cups reduced-fat (2%) milk

1¾ lbs large potatoes

1 oz Parmesan cheese

2½ oz Gorgonzola cheese

1 tablespoon green pesto, to serve

Preheat the oven to 350°F. Snap the woody ends off the asparagus. Finely chop the bottom 1¼ inches of each stalk (reserving the rest). Peel and finely chop the onions. Put the chopped veg into a large non-stick pan on a medium heat with 2 tablespoons of olive oil. Cook for 15 minutes, or until softened, stirring regularly. Stir in the flour, then gradually stir in the milk. Simmer and stir for 5 minutes, blend until smooth (in batches, if needed), then return to the pan. Scrub and finely slice the potatoes, stir into the sauce and simmer on a low heat for another 5 minutes, stirring regularly. Finely grate in the Parmesan and season to perfection. Halve the remaining asparagus lengthways, leaving any thin stalks whole.

Get a nice baking dish (roughly 12 x 10 inches) and spoon in enough sauce and potatoes to cover the base. Sprinkle over a few pieces of asparagus and a few bombs of Gorgonzola, then repeat until you've used up all the ingredients, finishing with asparagus and a little sauce. Bake for 1 hour, or until golden, bubbling and the potatoes are tender. Let it sit for 10 minutes, then dollop with pesto to serve.

ENERGY	FAT	SAT FAT	PROTEIN	CARBS	SUGARS	SALT	FIBER
378kcal	15.4g	6g	17.8g	44.8g	14.8g	0.8g	3.4g

MY RUSSIAN POTATO SALAD

BABY CORNICHONS, APPLES, CARROTS, PEAS & CHIVES

SERVES 8 AS A SIDE | TOTAL 25 MINUTES

1¾ lbs new potatoes

14 oz carrots

7 oz frozen peas

8 heaping tablespoons plain yogurt

2 heaping teaspoons grainy mustard

3½ oz mixed baby cornichons
   & pickled onions

2 eating apples

½ a bunch of chives (½ oz)

Scrub the potatoes and carrots, then dice into ¾-inch chunks. Cook in a large pan of boiling salted water for 10 minutes, or until soft, adding the peas for the last 2 minutes. Meanwhile, to make the dressing, put the yogurt and mustard into a large bowl with 1 tablespoon of red wine vinegar. Finely chop and mix in the cornichons and pickled onions. Add 2 tablespoons of starchy cooking water from the potatoes, then scoop out a few pieces of cooked potato, mash well and mix through the dressing to make it extra creamy. Season to perfection.

Drain the veg and leave to steam dry while you core the apples and dice into ¾-inch chunks. Finely chop most of the chives and stir half into the dressing with the apples, potatoes, peas and carrots. Sprinkle over the remaining chives and drizzle with 1 tablespoon of extra virgin olive oil, to finish.

ENERGY	FAT	SAT FAT	PROTEIN	CARBS	SUGARS	SALT	FIBER
179kcal	4.5g	1.5g	6g	30.4g	11.8g	0.4g	4.3g

1 DOUBLE PEPPER CHICKEN
SWEET PEPPER CHICKPEAS & CRUNCHY PEPPER SALSA

2 STICKY MISO PEPPERS
TOFU, PINEAPPLE, RICE NOODLES & CRUSHED WASABI PEAS

3 CHORIZO, PEPPER & SHRIMP BAKE
BEAUTIFULLY FLUFFY RICE, GARLIC, PARSLEY, LEMON & YOGURT

4 PEPPER & CHICKEN JALFREZI TRAYBAKE
LOTS OF FRESH BAY, SOFT GARLIC, FRESH GREEN CHILI, SWEET ONION & YOGURT

5 SWEET PEPPER POTATO WEDGES
SCRAMBLED EGG, RED LEICESTER CHEESE, COTTAGE CHEESE & PARSLEY

6 STUFFED RED PEPPERS
AVOCADO, LIME & FETA CHEESE, QUICK BLACK BEAN & SMOKED HAM STEW

7 CHARRED PEPPER FAJITAS
WHITE BEANS, RED ONION, YELLOW PEPPER & SMOKED ALMOND SAUCE

PEPPERS

DOUBLE PEPPER CHICKEN
SWEET PEPPER CHICKPEAS & CRUNCHY PEPPER SALSA

SERVES 4 | TOTAL 35 MINUTES

3 red peppers

1 red onion

6 cloves of garlic

½ a bunch of basil (½ oz)

1 x 14-oz can of plum tomatoes

2 x 15-oz cans of chickpeas

4 x 5¼-oz skinless boneless
    chicken breasts

thick balsamic vinegar

Halve, seed and finely chop the peppers, then place half of them in a large non-stick frying pan on a medium heat with 1 tablespoon of olive oil. Peel and finely chop the onion, adding three-quarters of it to the pan. Peel, finely slice and add 2 cloves of garlic. Cook it all for 10 minutes, or until softened, stirring regularly. Meanwhile, for the salsa, mix the remaining chopped peppers and onion with ½ a tablespoon each of red wine vinegar and extra virgin olive oil. Pick, finely slice and mix in most of the basil leaves, then season to perfection.

Add 1 tablespoon of red wine vinegar to the pepper pan, then pour it all into a blender with the canned tomatoes. Blitz until silky smooth, then pour back into the pan, drain and tip in the chickpeas, stir and simmer for 15 minutes. Score the chicken breasts in a criss-cross fashion and place in a large non-stick frying pan on a medium heat with 1 tablespoon of oil and the remaining 4 unpeeled garlic cloves. Cook for 8 minutes, or until the chicken is golden, juicy and cooked through, turning halfway. Slice and serve on top of the chickpeas, sprinkled with the salsa, garlic and reserved basil leaves, then drizzle with thick balsamic vinegar, to finish.

ENERGY	FAT	SAT FAT	PROTEIN	CARBS	SUGARS	SALT	FIBER
439kcal	14.5g	2.6g	46.5g	31.8g	12g	0.2g	10g

STICKY MISO PEPPERS

TOFU, PINEAPPLE, RICE NOODLES & CRUSHED WASABI PEAS

SERVES 2 | **TOTAL 25 MINUTES**

1 x 8-oz can of pineapple rings in juice	4 cloves of garlic
9¾ oz extra firm tofu	3 oz rice vermicelli noodles
2 mixed-color peppers	¾ oz wasabi peas
4 scallions	2 heaping teaspoons red miso paste

Place the pineapple rings (reserving the juice) in a large dry non-stick frying pan on a medium heat. Cut the tofu into four chunks and add to the pan. Let it all gently char for 4 minutes, then turn, char on the other side and remove, leaving the pan on the heat. Seed the peppers, chop into ¾-inch chunks and place in the pan with ½ a tablespoon of olive oil, then reduce to a medium-low heat. Trim the scallions, chop the white halves into ¾-inch lengths and add to the pan, reserving the green tops. Peel, finely slice and add the garlic, then cook it all for 10 minutes, or until soft and charred, stirring regularly. Meanwhile, finely slice the green halves of the scallions. In a heatproof bowl, cover the noodles with boiling kettle water. In a pestle and mortar, pound the wasabi peas until fine.

Mix the miso paste into the reserved pineapple juice, then pour into the pepper pan with a splash of water. Let it sizzle for a minute, then return the tofu and pineapple to the pan to glaze. Drain the noodles, divide between your plates and spoon over the sticky miso peppers, followed by the tofu and pineapple. Sprinkle with the sliced green scallions and crushed wasabi peas, then tuck right in.

ENERGY	FAT	SAT FAT	PROTEIN	CARBS	SUGARS	SALT	FIBER
459kcal	12g	2.1g	18.4g	68.2g	25.2g	1.5g	4.7g

CHORIZO, PEPPER & SHRIMP BAKE

BEAUTIFULLY FLUFFY RICE, GARLIC, PARSLEY, LEMON & YOGURT

SERVES 4 | **TOTAL 40 MINUTES**

3 mixed-color peppers	1 cup basmati rice
½ a bunch of Italian parsley (½ oz)	11 oz raw peeled jumbo shrimp
1¾ oz chorizo	2 lemons
4 cloves of garlic	¼ cup plain yogurt

Preheat the oven to 425°F. Cut each pepper into four rings, removing the seeds, and place directly on the bars of the oven to soften for 15 minutes. Meanwhile, finely chop the parsley, stalks and all, putting the chopped leaves aside. Finely chop the chorizo and place in a 12-inch non-stick ovenproof pan on a medium-high heat with ½ a tablespoon of olive oil. Stir for 1 minute, until crisp, then peel and finely grate in the garlic, add the chopped parsley stalks, stir for another minute, then remove to a bowl, leaving the pan on the heat. Stir in 1 cup of rice and 2 cups of boiling kettle water, season with sea salt and black pepper, nestle in the softened pepper rings, cover and put into the oven for 15 minutes.

Add the shrimp to the chorizo mixture, finely grate in all the lemon zest, squeeze in the juice of 1 lemon, then mix together. When the time's up on the rice, remove the pan, uncover and sprinkle over the chorizo mixture, gently poking the shrimp into the rice. Return to the oven for a final 5 minutes, or until the shrimp are cooked through. Drizzle over 1 tablespoon of extra virgin olive oil, and sprinkle over the reserved chopped parsley leaves. Serve with the yogurt and the remaining zested lemon cut into wedges, for squeezing over.

ENERGY	FAT	SAT FAT	PROTEIN	CARBS	SUGARS	SALT	FIBER
423kcal	10.9g	3g	24.6g	60.1g	6.8g	1.4g	3.6g

PEPPER & CHICKEN JALFREZI TRAYBAKE

LOTS OF FRESH BAY, SOFT GARLIC, FRESH GREEN CHILI, SWEET ONION & YOGURT

SERVES 4 | **TOTAL 1 HOUR**

4 chicken thighs, skin on, bone in

8 cloves of garlic

2 fresh green chilies

3 red peppers

8 fresh bay leaves

1 heaping tablespoon jalfrezi curry paste

2 tablespoons onion marmalade

¼ cup plain yogurt

Preheat the oven to 350°F. Put a sturdy 14- x 10-inch roasting pan on a medium heat on the stove. Season the chicken thighs with a pinch of sea salt and black pepper, then place in the pan skin-side down with 1 tablespoon of olive oil. Peel the garlic cloves, halve and seed the chilies, then scatter into the pan. Tear the peppers into quarters, removing the seeds, and add to the pan.

Turn the chicken once golden, then add the bay leaves, jalfrezi paste and onion marmalade, moving it all around with tongs to coat. Let it sizzle over the heat for 5 minutes, then add 2 tablespoons of red wine vinegar and transfer to the oven for 45 minutes, or until the chicken is falling off the bone. Mash the soft garlic cloves into the juices, then ripple through the yogurt and serve.

ENERGY	FAT	SAT FAT	PROTEIN	CARBS	SUGARS	SALT	FIBER
316kcal	19.5g	4.8g	20.7g	14.6g	11.6g	1.1g	3.2g

SWEET PEPPER POTATO WEDGES
SCRAMBLED EGG, RED LEICESTER CHEESE, COTTAGE CHEESE & PARSLEY

SERVES 4 | TOTAL 1 HOUR

2 lbs potatoes	1 bunch of Italian parsley (1 oz)
2 onions	4 large eggs
2 cloves of garlic	¼ cup cottage cheese
4 mixed-color peppers	1½ oz red Leicester cheese or other English Cheddar

Preheat the oven to 400°F. Scrub the potatoes, chop lengthways into ¾-inch wedges, toss with 2 tablespoons of olive oil and a pinch of sea salt and black pepper, then arrange in a single layer in your largest roasting pan. Roast for 40 minutes, or until golden and cooked through, shaking halfway. Meanwhile, peel and finely slice the onions and garlic, and place in a large non-stick frying pan with 1 tablespoon of oil on a medium-low heat. Halve, seed, slice and add the peppers. Cook for 30 minutes, or until soft and sweet, stirring occasionally. When the time's almost up, add 2 tablespoons of red wine vinegar and season to perfection.

Finely chop the top leafy half of the parsley. Beat the eggs. Now, it's easiest to finish this off 2 portions at a time, so remove half the contents of the pan to a plate. Add half the wedges to the pan, pour in half the beaten egg, add a quarter of the parsley, then toss and stir it all vigorously over the heat until the egg is just lightly scrambled. Immediately plate up, spoon over half the cottage cheese, grate over half the red Leicester, sprinkle over another quarter of the parsley and let two lucky people tuck in while you crack on with the second set of portions.

ENERGY	FAT	SAT FAT	PROTEIN	CARBS	SUGARS	SALT	FIBER
489kcal	21.7g	5.9g	19.2g	58.5g	14.1g	1.1g	8.5g

STUFFED RED PEPPERS
AVOCADO, LIME & FETA CHEESE, QUICK BLACK BEAN & SMOKED HAM STEW

SERVES 4 | TOTAL 40 MINUTES

4 small red peppers

7 oz sliced smoked ham

1 onion

2 x 15-oz cans of black beans

1 x 8-oz package of mixed cooked grains

2 oz feta cheese

1 ripe avocado

2 limes

Preheat the oven to 400°F. Cut the lids off the peppers, pull out the seeds, then sit the lids and bases directly on the bars of the oven to start softening. Meanwhile, finely chop the ham and place in a large non-stick ovenproof frying pan on a medium heat with 1 tablespoon of olive oil, stirring regularly while you peel and finely chop the onion. Once the ham is crispy, stir in the onion and cook for 5 minutes, or until softened, stirring regularly. Add 1 tablespoon of red wine vinegar, then pour in the beans, juice and all. Remove the peppers from the oven and nestle the bases into the stew. Divide the grains and a little feta between them and sit the pepper lids ajar. Transfer to the oven for 20 minutes, or until the peppers are cooked through, then season the stew to perfection.

Halve, pit, scoop out and dice the avocado, then toss with the juice of 1 lime and a pinch of seasoning. Spoon the avocado over the cooked peppers, crumble over the rest of the feta, and serve with lime wedges, for squeezing over.

ENERGY	FAT	SAT FAT	PROTEIN	CARBS	SUGARS	SALT	FIBER
454kcal	19g	5.2g	27.4g	36.9g	11.6g	1.7g	18.9g

CHARRED PEPPER FAJITAS

WHITE BEANS, RED ONION, YELLOW PEPPER & SMOKED ALMOND SAUCE

SERVES 2 | **TOTAL 35 MINUTES**

3 mixed-color peppers

1 lime

1 oz smoked almonds

2 red onions

1 x 15-oz can of cannellini beans

4 corn tortillas

2 tablespoons cottage cheese

½ a bunch of cilantro (½ oz)

Put a large non-stick frying pan on a high heat. Seed and finely chop the yellow pepper. Place in the pan to lightly char for 3 minutes while you squeeze the lime juice into a blender with ½ a tablespoon of red wine vinegar, half the almonds and ⅔ cup of water. Add the charred yellow pepper, season and blitz until smooth.

Slice the remaining peppers into ½-inch rings, removing the seeds, and place in the hot pan. Peel the onions, slice into ½-inch-thick rounds, add to the pan and cook it all for 10 minutes, or until soft and charred, stirring regularly. Pour in the beans, juice and all, followed by the yellow pepper sauce. Let it bubble and reduce for 5 minutes, or until thick, then season to perfection. Chop or crush the remaining almonds. Warm the tortillas, spoon over the pepper and bean mixture and the cottage cheese, tear over the cilantro leaves, and sprinkle with the crushed almonds, to finish.

ENERGY	FAT	SAT FAT	PROTEIN	CARBS	SUGARS	SALT	FIBER
581kcal	14.5g	2g	23.8g	84.8g	25.7g	1g	19.5g

1 SHRIMP TOAST TOASTIE
SCALLIONS, GINGER, SESAME & SWEET CHILI SAUCE

2 FRAGRANT SHRIMP BALLS
EASY DUMPLINGS, ASPARAGUS, FRESH CHILI & BROTH

3 GARLIC SHRIMP KEBABS
SWEET GRILLED PEPPERS, BREAD, FETA CHEESE & QUICK TOMATO SAUCE

4 SPICY SHRIMP NOODLES
BOK CHOY, GINGER, GARLIC, CHILI JAM & SESAME SEEDS

5 EASY SHRIMP CURRY
GARLIC, GINGER, FRESH CHILI & SIMPLE FLUFFY RICE CAKE

6 CREAMY SHRIMP LINGUINE
SMOKED PANCETTA, GARLIC, ARUGULA & A KISS OF RED WINE

7 SHRIMP POKE BOWL
CREAMY MINT DRESSING, GRAINS, MANGO & AVOCADO

SHRIMP

SHRIMP TOAST TOASTIE
SCALLIONS, GINGER, SESAME & SWEET CHILI SAUCE

SERVES 2 | TOTAL 20 MINUTES

2 scallions

5½ oz raw peeled jumbo shrimp

¾-inch piece of fresh ginger

½ tablespoon reduced-sodium
    soy sauce

1 large egg

4 slices of white bread

2 tablespoons raw sesame seeds

1 tablespoon sweet chili sauce

On a large board, trim the scallions, then finely chop with most of the shrimp (save four for later). Peel and finely grate over the ginger, add the soy and the egg yolk (reserving the white), then chop and mix it all together. Divide and spread the filling between two slices of bread, then sandwich the other slices on top.

Now, you can use a panini press or a non-stick frying pan – either way, get it hot. Brush both sides of each sandwich with the egg white, pat on the sesame seeds, then halve the remaining shrimp and press into the bread on one side only. Place in your panini press for 3 minutes, or put in the pan with 1 teaspoon of olive oil and a weight on top of the sandwich to toast for 2½ minutes on each side, or until golden and cooked through. Slice and serve with sweet chili sauce for dipping, or you could even brush the sauce over your toastie for added joy.

ENERGY	FAT	SAT FAT	PROTEIN	CARBS	SUGARS	SALT	FIBER
366kcal	11.2g	2.4g	25.1g	40.6g	7.2g	1.8g	2.7g

FRAGRANT SHRIMP BALLS

EASY DUMPLINGS, ASPARAGUS, FRESH CHILI & BROTH

SERVES 2 | TOTAL 20 MINUTES

heaping ¾ cup self-rising flour

2 cloves of garlic

1½-inch piece of fresh ginger

½ a bunch of cilantro (½ oz)

5½ oz raw peeled jumbo shrimp

5½ oz fine asparagus

2 cups fresh chicken stock

1 fresh red chili

Mix the flour with 3 tablespoons of water and 1 tablespoon of olive oil, then knead until it just comes together as a smooth dough (don't overwork it). Cover and put aside. On a board, peel and finely slice the garlic. Peel and finely matchstick the ginger. Finely chop the cilantro stalks (reserving the leaves). Pile the shrimp on top, then chop and mix it all into a rough paste. Divide into eight and shape into balls, then divide and shape the dough into eight dumplings. Snap the woody ends off the asparagus, then chop each stalk into three.

Bring the stock to a boil in a shallow pan. Plop in the dumplings, cover and simmer for 3 minutes. Add the shrimp balls and simmer for 2 minutes, followed by the chopped asparagus for a final 1 minute. Season the broth to perfection. Finely slice the chili, and scatter over with the cilantro leaves. Divide between warm bowls and serve each portion drizzled with 1 teaspoon of extra virgin olive oil.

ENERGY	FAT	SAT FAT	PROTEIN	CARBS	SUGARS	SALT	FIBER
369kcal	11.1g	1.8g	28g	41.6g	2.9g	1.7g	3.2g

GARLIC SHRIMP KEBABS
SWEET GRILLED PEPPERS, BREAD, FETA CHEESE & QUICK TOMATO SAUCE

SERVES 2 | TOTAL 25 MINUTES

2¾ oz good sourdough bread

5½ oz raw peeled jumbo shrimp

½ x 16-oz jar of roasted red peppers

3 cloves of garlic

½ a bunch of Italian parsley (½ oz)

1 lemon

1 x 14-oz can of cherry tomatoes

¾ oz feta cheese

Preheat the broiler to high. Slice the bread ½ inch thick, then cut into 1¼-inch chunks and place in a large bowl with the shrimp. Drain the peppers, slice 1¼ inches thick lengthways and add to the bowl. Peel the garlic. Finely chop 1 clove and add to the bowl, then finely slice the other 2 and put aside. Finely chop the parsley, stalks and all, and add to the mix. Finely grate in the lemon zest, squeeze in half the juice, add 1 tablespoon of olive oil and a pinch of black pepper and mix well. Take pride in skewering up the shrimp and bread on 2 skewers, interlacing with the peppers, and don't pack it all on too tightly. Sit each skewer across a roasting pan and broil for 6 to 8 minutes, turning halfway – keep an eye on them!

Meanwhile, put a non-stick frying pan on a medium heat with ½ a tablespoon of olive oil and the sliced garlic. Stir regularly for 2 minutes, or until lightly golden, then pour in the canned tomatoes to bubble away until the skewers are ready, squashing a few with the back of your spoon. Add a squeeze of lemon juice, then season the sauce to perfection. Serve the kebabs on top of the sauce, sprinkled with feta and black pepper, then finish with 1 teaspoon of extra virgin olive oil.

ENERGY	FAT	SAT FAT	PROTEIN	CARBS	SUGARS	SALT	FIBER
354kcal	16g	3.6g	22.9g	29.4g	11.6g	1.1g	3.8g

SPICY SHRIMP NOODLES

BOK CHOY, GINGER, GARLIC, CHILI JAM & SESAME SEEDS

SERVES 1 | **TOTAL 10 MINUTES**

1 bok choy

1 clove of garlic

¾-inch piece of fresh ginger

2¾ oz fine egg noodles

3 oz raw peeled jumbo shrimp

1 heaping teaspoon raw sesame seeds

1 heaping teaspoon chili jam or red pepper jelly

2 teaspoons reduced-sodium soy sauce

Finely slice the bok choy, putting the leaves aside. Char the base slices in a dry non-stick frying pan on a medium-high heat while you peel and finely slice the garlic, then peel and finely grate the ginger. Cook the noodles in a pan of boiling water according to the package instructions, adding the bok choy leaves for the last 10 seconds. Alongside, stir-fry the garlic, ginger, shrimp, sesame seeds, chili jam and 1 tablespoon of olive oil with the charred bok choy slices.

Pour the soy into a serving bowl. As soon as the shrimp are pink, spoon everything from the pan into the bowl, then use tongs to drag in the noodles and bok choy leaves with a few splashes of cooking water. Twist and toss it all together well, taste and check the seasoning, then devour.

ENERGY	FAT	SAT FAT	PROTEIN	CARBS	SUGARS	SALT	FIBER
600kcal	24.1g	4.3g	28g	67.4g	9.4g	1.7g	2.5g

EASY SHRIMP CURRY

GARLIC, GINGER, FRESH CHILI & A SIMPLE FLUFFY RICE CAKE

SERVES 4 | **TOTAL 20 MINUTES**

1 cup basmati rice	1 bunch of scallions
4 cloves of garlic	2 tablespoons mango chutney
1 fresh red chili	11 oz raw peeled jumbo shrimp
1½-inch piece of fresh ginger	⅔ cup plain yogurt

Put 1 cup of rice and 2 cups of boiling kettle water into a medium non-stick pan with a pinch of sea salt. Boil for 10 minutes, then reduce to a low heat for 5 minutes, after which you'll be able to turn it out as a rice cake.

Meanwhile, peel the garlic and finely slice with the chili. Peel and matchstick the ginger. Trim the scallions and slice into ¾-inch lengths. Put it all into a large non-stick frying pan on a high heat with 1 tablespoon of olive oil, and stir-fry for 3 minutes, then stir in the mango chutney. Carefully pour half the mixture into a blender, returning the pan to the heat and adding the shrimp to stir-fry. Add ½ a cup of water to the blender, blitz until smooth, then pour straight back into the shrimp pan. Let it bubble and thicken slightly for 3 minutes, then, off the heat, ripple through the yogurt. Serve the curry on top of your fluffy rice cake.

ENERGY	FAT	SAT FAT	PROTEIN	CARBS	SUGARS	SALT	FIBER
253kcal	2.5g	1.2g	19.1g	40.8g	8.1g	1.4g	0.5g

CREAMY SHRIMP LINGUINE

SMOKED PANCETTA, GARLIC, ARUGULA & A KISS OF RED WINE

SERVES 2 | TOTAL 15 MINUTES

5 ¼ oz dried linguine

2 cloves of garlic

5 ½ oz raw peeled jumbo shrimp

4 slices of smoked pancetta or bacon

3 tablespoons Italian red wine

1 heaping tablespoon
   mascarpone cheese

1 ¾ oz arugula

½ oz Parmesan cheese

Cook the pasta in a pan of boiling salted water according to the package instructions. Meanwhile, peel and finely slice the garlic. Run your knife down the back of 2 shrimp, so they'll butterfly as they cook, then finely chop the rest.

Put a large non-stick frying pan on a medium heat. Finely slice the pancetta, sprinkle into the pan with 1 tablespoon of olive oil and fry until lightly golden. Toss in the garlic and whole shrimp for 2 minutes, then go in with the wine and let it cook away. Toss through the chopped shrimp and mascarpone for 1 minute, then use tongs to drag the pasta straight into the pan, letting a little starchy cooking water go with it. Roughly chop the arugula, add most of it to the pan and toss it all together over the heat until you have a silky sauce. Subtly season to perfection with the Parmesan and black pepper. Serve sprinkled with the remaining arugula and an extra grating of Parmesan, if you like.

ENERGY	FAT	SAT FAT	PROTEIN	CARBS	SUGARS	SALT	FIBER
514kcal	19.1g	7.5g	28.3g	56.3g	3.2g	0.9g	2.6g

SHRIMP POKE BOWL

CREAMY MINT DRESSING, GRAINS, MANGO & AVOCADO

SERVES 2 | TOTAL 20 MINUTES

½ a bunch of mint (½ oz)

6 tablespoons cottage cheese

5¼ oz cooked peeled jumbo shrimp

1 x 8-oz package of mixed cooked
    grains

½ a small ripe avocado

1 carrot

1 small ripe mango

3½ oz radishes

This is a bit of an assembly job, and that's the beauty of it. Start by tearing most of the top leafy half of the mint into a blender (saving a few pretty leaves). Add 4 tablespoons of cottage cheese, ½ a tablespoon of extra virgin olive oil and a splash of water. Blitz until smooth, season to perfection and toss with the shrimp.

Warm the grains according to the package instructions, dress with a little red wine vinegar and ½ a tablespoon of oil, then divide between serving bowls. Scoop out and finely slice the avocado, then divide and fan out on top of each portion. Peel the carrot into ribbons, pit, peel and dice the mango, finely slice the radishes, and divide up. Place your dressed shrimp proudly on top, spoon over the remaining cottage cheese, then sprinkle over your reserved mint leaves. Finish with a drizzle of extra virgin olive oil, then mix and dress as you like.

ENERGY	FAT	SAT FAT	PROTEIN	CARBS	SUGARS	SALT	FIBER
484kcal	18.7g	5.1g	26.9g	51.1g	13.2g	1.3g	5.8g

1 CULLEN SKINK FISHCAKES
SMOKED HADDOCK, CREAMY CHIVE & ONION SAUCE, LEMON

2 GOLDEN PARMESAN FISH BAKE
SWEET LEEKS, CRISPY SAGE, GARLIC, MUSTARD & LIMA BEANS

3 SPAGHETTI-WRAPPED FISH
SUN-DRIED TOMATO PESTO, SPINACH, CRÈME FRAÎCHE & BACON BITS

4 MY SPICY ETHIOPIAN FISH CURRY
BERBERE SPICE, SWEET ONION & TOMATO, FAST FLATBREADS & SPINACH

5 CHEAT'S FISH & CHIPS
BACON CRUMB, SMASHED PEAS & QUICK MINT SAUCE

6 SICILIAN FISH PASTA
GARLIC, CAPERS, OLIVES, ZUCCHINI & LEMON

7 QUICKEST WHITE FISH TAGINE
SWEET CHERRY TOMATOES, HARISSA, ASPARAGUS & FLUFFY COUSCOUS

WHITE FISH FILLET

CULLEN SKINK FISHCAKES

SMOKED HADDOCK, CREAMY CHIVE & ONION SAUCE, LEMON

SERVES 4 | TOTAL 45 MINUTES

2 lbs potatoes

1 onion

1 heaping tablespoon all-purpose flour

2½ cups reduced-fat (2%) milk

9¾ oz boneless smoked haddock

2 bunches of chives (1½ oz)

1 large egg

1 lemon

Peel the potatoes, chop into even-sized chunks and cook in a large pan of boiling salted water for 15 minutes, or until tender. Meanwhile, peel and finely chop the onion, place in a medium pan on a medium-low heat with 1 tablespoon of olive oil and cook for 10 minutes, or until softened, stirring regularly. Stir in the flour, gradually stir in the milk, and keep stirring until thickened. Gently poach the smoked haddock in the sauce for 5 minutes, making sure it's covered, then scoop out the fish and put aside, removing any skin. Finely chop the chives, then put one-quarter into a blender, pour in the sauce and blitz until silky smooth (in batches, if needed). Return to the pan and simmer on a low heat to the consistency of your liking.

Drain the potatoes and mash well, then beat and mix in the egg, with most of the remaining chives and a small pinch of sea salt and black pepper. Flake in the poached haddock, mix well, then divide into eight and shape into patties. Fry the fishcakes in 1 tablespoon of oil in a 12-inch non-stick frying pan on a medium heat for 5 minutes on each side, or until nicely golden and cooked through. Season the sauce to perfection and divide between your plates, then sit the fishcakes on top. Sprinkle with the remaining chives, drizzle with ½ a tablespoon of extra virgin olive oil and serve with lemon wedges, for squeezing over.

ENERGY	FAT	SAT FAT	PROTEIN	CARBS	SUGARS	SALT	FIBER
443kcal	11.7g	3.1g	26.6g	61.9g	11.5g	1.2g	4.4g

GOLDEN PARMESAN FISH BAKE

SWEET LEEKS, CRISPY SAGE, GARLIC, MUSTARD & LIMA BEANS

SERVES 4 | TOTAL 35 MINUTES

2 leeks

½ a bunch of sage (½ oz)

4 cloves of garlic

1 teaspoon grainy mustard

1 x 24-oz jar of lima beans

5¼ oz reduced-fat crème fraîche

4 x 5¼-oz white fish fillets,
    skin off, pin-boned

1 oz Parmesan cheese

Preheat the oven to 400°F. Trim the leeks, halve lengthways, wash, then slice ½ inch thick. Put a 12-inch shallow casserole pan on a medium-low heat with 2 tablespoons of olive oil. Pick in the sage leaves to get crispy, then scoop them out onto a plate, leaving the sage-infused oil behind. Stir in the leeks, then peel, finely slice and add the garlic, along with a splash of water. Cook for 10 minutes, or until soft, stirring occasionally. Stir in the mustard, followed by the lima beans (juice and all), crème fraîche and crispy sage. Mix well, then season to perfection. Nestle the fish into the beans, get it bubbling on the stove, then finely grate over the Parmesan. Transfer the pan to the oven for 10 minutes, or until golden and the fish is just cooked through.

ENERGY	FAT	SAT FAT	PROTEIN	CARBS	SUGARS	SALT	FIBER
354kcal	15.9g	6.4g	30g	22.8g	3.8g	0.4g	6g

SPAGHETTI-WRAPPED FISH

SUN-DRIED TOMATO PESTO, SPINACH, CRÈME FRAÎCHE & BACON BITS

SERVES 2 | TOTAL 25 MINUTES

2 oz dried spaghetti

2 x 4¼-oz white fish fillets, skin on, scaled, pin-boned

1 tablespoon sun-dried tomato pesto

2 small sprigs of rosemary

2 slices of smoked bacon

4 scallions

7 oz baby spinach

2 teaspoons reduced-fat crème fraîche

Preheat the broiler to high. Cook the spaghetti in a pan of boiling salted water according to the package instructions, then drain, running it under cold water to cool. Season the fish with sea salt and black pepper, then rub with the pesto. Divide the spaghetti into two, then wrap and knot it around the fish. Place on an oiled pan, turn the rosemary sprigs in the oil in the pan to coat and tuck them under the spaghetti. Broil for 10 minutes, or until golden and the fish is just cooked through.

Meanwhile, finely slice the bacon and place in a large non-stick frying pan on a medium heat to crisp up while you trim the scallions and slice them ½ inch thick. Spoon out the crispy bacon, leaving the pan on the heat, and go in with the scallions and 1 tablespoon of olive oil. Toss for 2 minutes, then add the spinach, stirring to wilt. Divide between your plates with the spaghetti-wrapped fish, then dollop over the crème fraîche and sprinkle with the crispy bacon bits. Drizzle over 1 teaspoon of extra virgin olive oil and finish with a pinch of black pepper.

ENERGY	FAT	SAT FAT	PROTEIN	CARBS	SUGARS	SALT	FIBER
342kcal	14.3g	3.3g	31.2g	23.6g	1.8g	1.8g	2.2g

MY SPICY ETHIOPIAN FISH CURRY

BERBERE SPICE, SWEET ONION & TOMATO, FAST FLATBREADS & SPINACH

SERVES 2 | TOTAL 20 MINUTES

1 lemon

1 heaping cup self-rising flour

2 cloves of garlic

2 tablespoons onion marmalade

2 teaspoons berbere spice mix

1 x 14-oz can of plum tomatoes

2 x 5¼-oz white fish fillets, skin off, pin-boned

1¾ oz baby spinach

Use a vegetable peeler to peel off thin strips of lemon zest and put aside. For the flatbreads, pile the flour into a bowl, then whisk in 1¼ cups of cold water. Squeeze in half the lemon juice and quickly beat until smooth. Place a medium non-stick frying pan on a medium-high heat with 1 tablespoon of olive oil. Peel, slice and add the garlic cloves, along with the strips of lemon zest. Stir for 2 minutes until lightly golden, then add the onion marmalade and the spice mix to bubble for 1 minute until sticky. Pour in the tomatoes, breaking them up with your spoon. Add the fish fillets, making sure they're covered by the sauce, and simmer on a low heat for 10 minutes, then flake up and stir through the fish.

Meanwhile, put an 8-inch non-stick frying pan on a medium-high heat. Spoon a ladleful of batter into the pan, then swirl it around and up the sides, pouring any excess back into the bowl. Cook for 2 minutes on one side only until just set and bubbly on top, and coming away from the sides, then ease out of the pan with a spatula, letting the pan cool slightly between flatbreads. Repeat, stacking them in a kitchen towel to keep warm. Toss the spinach with a squeeze of lemon juice and 1 teaspoon of extra virgin olive oil. Finish the curry with a squeeze of lemon juice and 1 teaspoon of oil, then season to perfection. Serve with the spinach and flatbreads.

ENERGY	FAT	SAT FAT	PROTEIN	CARBS	SUGARS	SALT	FIBER
509kcal	9.3g	1.3g	37.6g	73.4g	16.3g	1.6g	4.7g

CHEAT'S FISH & CHIPS
BACON CRUMB, SMASHED PEAS & QUICK MINT SAUCE

SERVES 4 | TOTAL 45 MINUTES

1¾ lbs potatoes

1 slice of smoked bacon

3½ oz stale bread

⅓ cup all-purpose flour

1 large egg

4 x 4½-oz white fish fillets, skin on, scaled, pin-boned

1 lb frozen peas

1 bunch of mint (1 oz)

Preheat the oven to 425°F. Scrub the potatoes, chop lengthways into ¾-inch wedges, toss with 1 tablespoon of olive oil and a pinch of sea salt and black pepper, then arrange in a single layer in your largest roasting pan. Roast for 40 minutes, or until golden and cooked through, shaking halfway. Meanwhile, roughly chop the bacon and place in a food processor, tear in the bread, add 1 tablespoon of oil and blitz into fine crumbs, then spread across a plate. Spread the flour across a second plate, and beat the egg on another. One by one, turn the fish in the flour, then the egg, letting any excess drip off, and finally turn in the bacon crumb. Line up on a baking sheet and roast for 15 minutes, or until golden.

Cook the peas in a pan of boiling salted water, then drain and mash well. Pick the mint leaves into a pestle and mortar, pound into a paste, then muddle in 1 tablespoon each of red wine vinegar and extra virgin olive oil, and season to perfection. Serve the fish and chips with the peas, dolloped with the mint sauce.

ENERGY	FAT	SAT FAT	PROTEIN	CARBS	SUGARS	SALT	FIBER
555kcal	14.7g	2.4g	39.1g	69.5g	9.1g	1.1g	10.2g

SICILIAN FISH PASTA

GARLIC, CAPERS, OLIVES, ZUCCHINI & LEMON

SERVES 2 | TOTAL 15 MINUTES

8 oz fresh lasagne sheets

1 zucchini

2 cloves of garlic

½ a bunch of Italian parsley (½ oz)

6 green olives

2 x 5¼-oz white fish fillets, skin off, pin-boned

1 heaping teaspoon baby capers

2 lemons

First up, get prepped. Stack up the lasagne sheets and, using a large sharp knife, carefully slice into very fine strips. Chop the zucchini into fine matchsticks or coarsely grate it. Peel the garlic and finely slice with the parsley, stalks and all. Crush and pit the olives, tearing up the flesh. Cut the fish into ½-inch chunks.

Put a large non-stick frying pan on a high heat with 1 tablespoon of olive oil. Go in with the garlic, parsley, olives and capers, stirring regularly until the garlic is lightly golden. Toss in the fish and zucchini and cook for 3 minutes. Alongside, cook the pasta in boiling salted water for 3 minutes, then use tongs to drag it straight into the frying pan, letting a splash of pasta cooking water go with it. Toss over the heat for just 30 seconds, squeeze in the lemon juice, season with black pepper, drizzle with 1 tablespoon of extra virgin olive oil and serve right away.

ENERGY	FAT	SAT FAT	PROTEIN	CARBS	SUGARS	SALT	FIBER
416kcal	16.3g	4.3g	23.6g	44.4g	4.2g	0.5g	1g

QUICKEST WHITE FISH TAGINE

SWEET CHERRY TOMATOES, HARISSA, ASPARAGUS & FLUFFY COUSCOUS

SERVES 2 | TOTAL 15 MINUTES

1 cup couscous

4 cloves of garlic

8 oz ripe mixed-color cherry
   tomatoes

8 oz asparagus

2 heaping teaspoons rose harissa

2 x 5¼-oz white fish fillets, skin off,
   pin-boned

1 lemon

2 tablespoons plain yogurt

Place the couscous in a bowl, add a pinch of sea salt and black pepper, then just cover with boiling kettle water, and cover. Peel and slice the garlic, then place in a shallow casserole pan on a medium-high heat with 1 tablespoon of olive oil, stirring while you halve the cherry tomatoes, adding them to the pan as you go. Snap the woody ends off the asparagus, roughly chop the spears and stir into the pan, then season with salt and pepper. Rub most of the harissa over the fish, sit it on top of the veg, finely grate over the lemon zest and squeeze over half the juice. Add ⅔ cup of water, cover and cook for 5 minutes, or until the fish is just cooked through.

Fluff up the couscous. Ripple the remaining harissa through the yogurt, then spoon it over the fish and couscous. Serve with lemon wedges, for squeezing over.

ENERGY	FAT	SAT FAT	PROTEIN	CARBS	SUGARS	SALT	FIBER
560kcal	13.4g	2.2g	43.5g	70.2g	10.9g	1.5g	4.9g

1 SESAME ROAST CHICKEN
KIMCHI & SILKEN TOFU CRUNCHY VEG SLAW & FLUFFY RICE

2 FARMHOUSE ROAST CHICKEN
GARLIC MUSHROOMS & BACON, SPINACH & CRÈME FRAÎCHE LENTILS

3 ROAST CHICKEN MARGHERITA
GIANT STUFFED ROASTED GNOCCHI, ROASTED TOMATOES, GARLIC & ARUGULA

4 MY EASY PIRI PIRI CHICKEN
GARLIC, SMOKED PAPRIKA, HARISSA, MINT & CHUNKY POTATO WEDGES

5 CUMBERLAND ROAST CHICKEN
ROAST POTATO, PARSNIP, LEEK & SAGE TRAYBAKE, PEAR & WATERCRESS

6 HOISIN ROAST CHICKEN
STEAMED PANCAKES, GARNISHES & DIPPING SAUCE

7 HARISSA ROAST CHICKEN
CHUNKY SWEET POTATOES & AMAZING CHICKPEA FLATBREADS

WHOLE
CHICKEN

SESAME ROAST CHICKEN

KIMCHI & SILKEN TOFU CRUNCHY VEG SLAW & FLUFFY RICE

SERVES 6 | TOTAL 1 HOUR 30 MINUTES

10 oz kimchi	10 oz silken tofu
1½-inch piece of fresh ginger	2 oz raw sesame seeds
1 x 3-lb whole chicken	1 cup basmati rice
2 tablespoons liquid honey	2 x 10-oz packages of mixed stir-fry veg

Preheat the oven to 350°F. In a blender, blitz the kimchi, peeled ginger, 1 tablespoon each of red wine vinegar and olive oil and 6 tablespoons of water until very smooth. In a roasting pan, rub one-third of the kimchi dressing all over the chicken, getting into all the nooks and crannies. Pour ⅔ cup of water into the pan, then roast for 1 hour 20 minutes, or until golden and cooked through. Halfway through, add another ⅔ cup of water, baste with the juices and scrape up any sticky bits. Spoon another third of the dressing into a small bowl, mix with the honey and put aside. Drain the tofu and blitz with the rest of the dressing in the blender. Toast the sesame seeds in a non-stick frying pan until lightly golden, then set aside.

With 10 minutes to go, put 1 cup of rice, 2 cups of boiling kettle water and a pinch of sea salt into a medium pan. Cover and cook on a medium heat for 12 minutes, or until all the water has been absorbed. Remove the chicken from the oven, lift it up with tongs and slide a rack underneath it so it sits over the pan. Pour and brush the honey dressing all over the chicken, then sprinkle with the sesame seeds. Move the rice and chicken to a serving platter, then stir 1 tablespoon of vinegar into the pan. Tip in the mixed veg and half the tofu dressing to coat. Serve the rest in a bowl on the side, drizzled with 1 teaspoon of extra virgin olive oil.

ENERGY	FAT	SAT FAT	PROTEIN	CARBS	SUGARS	SALT	FIBER
612kcal	28.2g	6.3g	43.9g	48g	9.1g	4.3g	1.3g

FARMHOUSE ROAST CHICKEN

GARLIC MUSHROOMS & BACON, SPINACH & CRÈME FRAÎCHE LENTILS

SERVES 6 | TOTAL 1 HOUR 30 MINUTES

1 x 3-lb whole chicken	8 oz baby spinach
1 bulb of garlic	2 x 15-oz cans of green lentils
3 slices of smoked bacon	3½ oz reduced-fat crème fraîche
1½ lbs mixed mushrooms	½ a bunch of tarragon (½ oz)

Preheat the oven to 350°F. Sit the chicken and garlic bulb in a large sturdy roasting pan, sprinkle with a pinch of sea salt and black pepper, drizzle with 1 tablespoon each of red wine vinegar and olive oil and rub all over the bird. Roast for 1 hour.

Take the pan out of the oven and use tongs to move the chicken to a plate, laying the bacon over the breasts. Use a potato masher to squash and squeeze the soft garlic out of the skins in the pan, then toss the mushrooms in the juices, tearing any larger ones. Return the pan to the oven. Sit the chicken directly on the bars above and roast for another 20 minutes, or until everything is golden and cooked through.

Use a slotted spoon to transfer the garlicky mushrooms to a serving platter, sitting the chicken on top to rest. Place the pan of juices on a high heat on the stove, add the spinach, then drain and add the lentils. Stir until the spinach has wilted, then, off the heat, ripple through the crème fraîche and season to perfection. Pick the tarragon leaves over the chicken, and serve it all together.

ENERGY	FAT	SAT FAT	PROTEIN	CARBS	SUGARS	SALT	FIBER
419kcal	22g	7g	42.3g	13.1g	1.5g	0.8g	6.2g

ROAST CHICKEN MARGHERITA

GIANT STUFFED ROASTED GNOCCHI, ROASTED TOMATOES, GARLIC & ARUGULA

SERVES 6 | **TOTAL 1 HOUR 40 MINUTES**

3 lbs floury potatoes

3 lbs ripe tomatoes

2 bulbs of garlic

1 bunch of basil (1 oz)

1 x 3-lb whole chicken

⅓ cup all-purpose flour

7 oz ball of smoked mozzarella

2 oz arugula

Preheat the oven to 350°F. Scrub the potatoes, chop into even-sized chunks and cook in a large pan of boiling salted water for 15 minutes, or until tender. Halve the tomatoes and place in a large roasting pan. Break in the unpeeled garlic cloves. Pick a few pretty basil leaves for later, then stuff the rest of the bunch into the chicken cavity and add the chicken to the pan. Season with sea salt and black pepper, drizzle everything with 2 tablespoons each of red wine vinegar and olive oil, then toss well, rubbing all that flavor into the bird. Sit the chicken directly on the bars of the oven and put the pan of tomatoes beneath it. Roast for 1 hour 20 minutes, or until the chicken is golden and cooked through.

Meanwhile, drain the potatoes, steam dry, mash, season and mix with the flour. As soon as it's cool enough to handle, divide and roll into 12 equal balls. Cut the smoked mozzarella into 12 chunks, poke one chunk into each ball, and seal. Place all the balls on an oiled 14- x 10-inch baking sheet and roast at the bottom of the oven for the remaining 1 hour, or until golden. Remove the chicken to the pan of tomatoes and allow to rest, then squeeze a few garlic cloves out of their skins and mash into the pan juices. Sprinkle over the reserved basil leaves, then serve with the giant gnocchi and arugula, drizzling the garlicky juices over everything. Joy.

ENERGY	FAT	SAT FAT	PROTEIN	CARBS	SUGARS	SALT	FIBER
714kcal	27.5g	9.1g	46.5g	66.1g	10.3g	1.1g	8.6g

MY EASY PIRI PIRI CHICKEN

GARLIC, SMOKED PAPRIKA, HARISSA, MINT & CHUNKY POTATO WEDGES

SERVES 6 | TOTAL 1 HOUR 30 MINUTES

2 onions

10 fresh mixed-color chilies

1 bulb of garlic

2 tablespoons rose harissa

1 heaping teaspoon smoked paprika

1 x 3-lb whole chicken

2½ lbs potatoes

4 sprigs of mint

Preheat the oven to 350°F. Peel and quarter the onions and place in a large roasting pan. Prick and add the whole chilies. Halve the unpeeled garlic bulb across the middle and add to the pan with the harissa, paprika, a pinch of sea salt and black pepper, 2 tablespoons of red wine vinegar and 1 tablespoon of olive oil. Use a large sharp knife to carefully cut down the back of the chicken, so you can open it out flat. Add to the pan and toss well, rubbing all that flavor into the bird. Place the chicken, breast-side up, directly on the top bars of the oven with the pan of onions beneath it. Roast for 1 hour, or until the chicken is golden and cooked through. Scrub the potatoes, chop lengthways into chunky wedges, toss with 1 tablespoon of oil and a pinch of seasoning, then arrange in a single layer in your largest roasting pan and place in the oven below the onions.

After 30 minutes, remove the onion pan from the oven, basting the chicken with any juices from the pan. Shake the wedges and move up to sit under the chicken for the remaining 30 minutes. For the sauce, halve and seed the chilies, squeeze half the soft garlic flesh out of the skins, then blitz both in a blender with the onions and all the tasty juices from the pan, half the mint leaves and 1 tablespoon of red wine vinegar until smooth, adding a good splash of water, if needed, then season to perfection. Serve the chicken with the wedges and piri piri sauce, scattered with the rest of the mint leaves and roasted garlic.

ENERGY	FAT	SAT FAT	PROTEIN	CARBS	SUGARS	SALT	FIBER
501kcal	20.9g	4.9g	38.4g	42.2g	6.4g	0.8g	4.3g

CUMBERLAND ROAST CHICKEN

ROAST POTATO, PARSNIP, LEEK & SAGE TRAYBAKE, PEAR & WATERCRESS

SERVES 6 | **TOTAL 1 HOUR 45 MINUTES**

2½ lbs potatoes

2 parsnips

2 leeks

½ a bunch of sage (½ oz)

3 Cumberland or other good-quality, herby pork sausages

1 x 3-lb whole chicken

1 pear

3 oz watercress

Preheat the oven to 350°F. Scrub the potatoes and finely slice, then wash, trim and finely slice the parsnips and leeks. Place it all in a 16- x 12-inch roasting pan, and toss with 2 tablespoons of olive oil, a pinch of sea salt and black pepper and the sage leaves (reserving the stalks and a few leaves for later). Squeeze the sausagemeat out of the skins and scrunch together. Pull up the chicken skin at the tip of the breasts and use a spatula to gently separate the skin down the breast meat, then poke half the sausagemeat into each side, smoothing it out as you go. Secure the skin with a cocktail stick. Rub the chicken all over with a pinch of salt and pepper and 1 tablespoon of oil. Stuff the sage stalks into the chicken cavity. Place the chicken directly on the bars of the oven with the pan of veg underneath, and roast for 1 hour 20 minutes, or until everything is golden and cooked through.

With 10 minutes to go, sprinkle the reserved sage leaves over the pan of veg, so they crisp up nicely. Very finely slice or coarsely grate the pear, and toss with the watercress. Sit the chicken on the veg and serve everything together at the table.

ENERGY	FAT	SAT FAT	PROTEIN	CARBS	SUGARS	SALT	FIBER
608kcal	28.6g	7.4g	43.7g	46.6g	8.2g	1.4g	6.9g

HOISIN ROAST CHICKEN

STEAMED PANCAKES, GARNISHES & DIPPING SAUCE

SERVES 6 | **TOTAL 1 HOUR 30 MINUTES**

1 x 3-lb whole chicken

8 tablespoons hoisin sauce

1 clementine

4 fresh mixed-color chilies

1 bunch of scallions

1 English cucumber

1 cup sprouting cress

30 Chinese pancakes

Preheat the oven to 350°F. Sit the chicken in a snug-fitting roasting pan. Pull up the skin at the tip of the breasts and use a spatula to gently separate the skin down the breast meat, then pour 2 tablespoons of hoisin sauce into each side, smoothing it out as you go. Secure the skin with a cocktail stick. Rub the chicken all over with a pinch of sea salt and black pepper and 1 tablespoon of olive oil. Halve the clementine and 1 chili, chop off 2 inches of green scallion tops, and place in the chicken cavity. Roast for 1 hour 20 minutes, or until golden and cooked through.

Meanwhile, trim the remaining scallions, then finely slice lengthways with the remaining chilies and put into a bowl of cold water to curl up. Matchstick the cucumber. Snip the cress. Steam the pancakes according to the package instructions (or, if you're feeling adventurous and want to make your own from scratch, check out the recipe at jamieoliver.com/chinesepancakes). Remove the chicken to a platter, mix any lovely pan juices with the remaining hoisin, for dipping, then serve with the pancakes and garnishes, and let everyone dig in.

ENERGY	FAT	SAT FAT	PROTEIN	CARBS	SUGARS	SALT	FIBER
475kcal	20.6g	4.8g	38.7g	33g	4.3g	0.6g	2.4g

HARISSA ROAST CHICKEN

CHUNKY SWEET POTATOES & AMAZING CHICKPEA FLATBREADS

SERVES 6 | **TOTAL 1 HOUR 40 MINUTES**

1 x 3-lb whole chicken

6 sweet potatoes (3 lbs total)

¼ cup rose harissa

1 bunch of mint (1 oz)

1 x 15-oz can of chickpeas

2 cups whole-grain self-rising flour, plus extra for dusting

½ a red cabbage

10 oz cottage cheese

Preheat the oven to 350°F. Sit the chicken in a large roasting pan, then scrub, halve and add the sweet potatoes. Spoon over the harissa, 1 tablespoon each of red wine vinegar and olive oil, and a pinch of sea salt and black pepper, then rub until everything is well coated. Put half the mint into the cavity of the chicken, then roast for 1 hour 20 minutes, or until everything is golden and cooked through.

Meanwhile, pour the chickpeas into a bowl, juice and all. Finely chop and add the rest of the mint leaves (reserving the pretty ones for later), tip in the flour and scrunch into a dough, adding a little more flour to bring it together, if needed. Knead on a flour-dusted surface for 2 minutes, then divide into six equal balls and roll each out to just under ½ inch thick. Fry two at a time in a large dry non-stick frying pan on a medium-high heat for 4 minutes per side, or until golden, then keep warm in the oven. Very finely slice or coarsely grate the red cabbage, then toss with a pinch of salt and 2 tablespoons of red wine vinegar. Serve the chicken and sweet potatoes with the pickled red cabbage and the chickpea flatbreads, sprinkled with the reserved mint leaves. Scrape up any sticky bits and a spoonful of nice juices from the pan, ripple through the cottage cheese and serve on the side.

ENERGY	FAT	SAT FAT	PROTEIN	CARBS	SUGARS	SALT	FIBER
517kcal	19.8g	5.1g	47.1g	39.3g	5.6g	1.4g	8.6g

1 CHEAT'S MUSHROOM RISOTTO
MIXED GRAINS, THYME, GARLIC, CRÈME FRAÎCHE & PARMESAN

2 MUSHROOM & CHICKEN CACCIATORE
ITALIAN RED WINE, SWEET PEPPER & TOMATO SAUCE, ROSEMARY & OLIVES

3 MUSHROOM CANNELLONI
SWEET LEEKS, ONIONS & CREAMY CHEDDAR CHEESE SAUCE

4 MUSHROOM TOAD-IN-THE-HOLE
CRISPY GARLIC, PORTER & ONION GRAVY SPIKED WITH ROSEMARY

5 BAKED MUSHROOM SOUP
BREAD, SWEET RED ONIONS, GARLIC, THYME & GRUYÈRE

6 MUSHROOM CACIO E PEPE
CLASSIC PASTA WITH PECORINO CHEESE, SPIKED WITH TRUFFLE OIL & LEMON

7 MUSHROOM & BEEF STIR-FRY
GIANT NOODLES, FRAGRANT GINGER, GARLIC, CHILI OIL, SOY & SCALLIONS

MUSHROOMS

CHEAT'S MUSHROOM RISOTTO
MIXED GRAINS, THYME, GARLIC, CRÈME FRAÎCHE & PARMESAN

SERVES 2 | **TOTAL 20 MINUTES**

1 onion

8 oz chestnut or cremini mushrooms

½ a bunch of thyme (½ oz)

1 clove of garlic

1 x 8-oz package of mixed cooked grains

1¼ cups veg or chicken stock

1½ oz Parmesan cheese

1 heaping tablespoon reduced-fat crème fraîche

Peel and finely chop the onion and place in a medium high-sided non-stick pan on a medium heat with ½ a tablespoon of olive oil. Trim the stalk and base off each mushroom, giving you a beautiful cross section (like you see in the picture). Finely chop the stalks and trimmings and add to the pan. Strip in half the thyme leaves, then cook for 10 minutes, or until soft, stirring regularly. Alongside, put a non-stick frying pan on a medium heat with ½ a tablespoon of oil. Add the mushrooms cap-side up and cook until golden without moving them (around 7 minutes). Peel and finely slice the garlic, and pick the remaining thyme leaves.

Tip the grains into the onion pan and feed it with stock for 5 minutes, stirring every minute or so, until you've got a nice, oozy consistency. Turn the whole golden mushrooms, sprinkle the garlic and remaining thyme into the pan and cook for 3 more minutes, shaking occasionally. Finely grate most of the Parmesan into the grains, stir in the crème fraîche, then season to perfection. Divide between your plates, spoon over and press in the golden mushrooms, sprinkle with the crispy garlic and thyme, then use a vegetable peeler to shave over the remaining Parmesan.

ENERGY	FAT	SAT FAT	PROTEIN	CARBS	SUGARS	SALT	FIBER
423kcal	18.8g	7.1g	17.1g	44.9g	7.3g	1.8g	7.8g

MUSHROOM & CHICKEN CACCIATORE

ITALIAN RED WINE, SWEET PEPPER & TOMATO SAUCE, ROSEMARY & OLIVES

SERVES 6 | TOTAL 1 HOUR 30 MINUTES

6 chicken thighs, skin off, bone out

6 large portobello mushrooms

2 red onions

1 x 16-oz jar of roasted red peppers

12 black olives, with pits

4 sprigs of fresh rosemary

¾ cup Italian red wine

2 x 14-oz cans of plum tomatoes

Preheat the oven to 350°F. Season the chicken with sea salt and black pepper, then put it in a large shallow casserole pan on a medium-high heat with 1 tablespoon of olive oil. Cook for 10 minutes, or until golden, turning regularly. Meanwhile, peel and tear up the mushrooms, peel and finely chop the onions, drain and tear up the peppers, then squash and pit the olives.

Remove the chicken to a plate, leaving the pan on the heat. Stir the mushrooms, onions, peppers and olives into the pan, then strip in the rosemary. Cook for 10 minutes, or until softened, stirring regularly. Pour in the wine and let it cook away, then add the tomatoes and ½ a can's worth of water, breaking up the tomatoes with your spoon. Bring to a boil, stir in the chicken and any juices, then transfer to the oven for 1 hour, or until the chicken is tender.

ENERGY	FAT	SAT FAT	PROTEIN	CARBS	SUGARS	SALT	FIBER
255kcal	10.8g	2.4g	23.6g	11g	9g	0.9g	3.2g

MUSHROOM CANNELLONI
SWEET LEEKS, ONIONS & CREAMY CHEDDAR CHEESE SAUCE

SERVES 6 | **TOTAL 1 HOUR 40 MINUTES**

2 small onions

2 cloves of garlic

2 leeks

1½ lbs chestnut or cremini
   mushrooms

½ cup all-purpose flour

4 cups reduced-fat (2%) milk

4 oz Cheddar cheese

8 oz dried cannelloni tubes

Preheat the oven to 350°F. Peel the onions and garlic, then pulse until very fine in a food processor. Tip into a large casserole pan on a medium-high heat with 1 tablespoon of olive oil. Trim, wash, pulse and add the leeks. Saving 2 mushrooms for later, pulse the rest and stir into the pan. Cook it all for 15 minutes, stirring regularly, then season to perfection and turn the heat off. Meanwhile, for the sauce, pour 3 tablespoons of oil into a separate pan on a medium heat. Whisk in the flour for 2 minutes, then gradually whisk in the milk. Simmer for 5 minutes, or until thickened, then grate in the cheese and season to perfection.

Pour one-third of the sauce into a 12- x 10-inch roasting pan. As soon as the filling is cool enough to work with, push both ends of each pasta tube into it to fill, lining them up in the pan as you go. Pour over the rest of the sauce, then finely slice the reserved mushrooms and use them to decorate the top. Drizzle with 1 tablespoon of oil and bake for 45 minutes, or until golden and cooked through.

ENERGY	FAT	SAT FAT	PROTEIN	CARBS	SUGARS	SALT	FIBER
489kcal	22.4g	8g	20.6g	53g	13g	0.7g	3.6g

MUSHROOM TOAD-IN-THE-HOLE

CRISPY GARLIC, PORTER & ONION GRAVY SPIKED WITH ROSEMARY

SERVES 4 | TOTAL 1 HOUR 15 MINUTES

4 large eggs

1 cup + 2 tablespoons
   all-purpose flour

¾ cup whole milk

4 large portobello mushrooms

2 onions

4 sprigs of rosemary

1 cup smooth porter beer

2 cloves of garlic

Preheat the oven to 400°F. Whisk the eggs, 1 cup of flour, a pinch of sea salt, the milk and 2 tablespoons of water into a smooth batter, then put aside.

Peel the mushrooms, saving the peelings. Place the mushrooms cap-side down in a large non-stick roasting pan, drizzle with 1 tablespoon of olive oil and season with salt and black pepper. Roast for 30 minutes. Meanwhile, for the gravy, peel the onions and finely slice with the mushroom peelings, then place in a pan on a medium-low heat with 2 tablespoons of oil. Strip in half the rosemary and cook for 15 minutes, or until dark and gnarly, stirring occasionally. Add the porter and 2 tablespoons of red wine vinegar and let it reduce by half, then stir in the remaining flour. Gradually add 2¾ cups of water, stirring regularly, then simmer to the consistency of your liking and season to perfection. Peel and finely slice the garlic, pick the remaining rosemary, then drizzle and rub it all with a little oil.

Remove the pan from the oven and put the mushrooms on a plate for a moment. Working quickly but carefully, pour the batter into the pan, sit the mushrooms toward the center, then sprinkle over the oiled garlic and rosemary. Return to the oven for 25 minutes, or until puffed up and golden. Serve with the gravy.

ENERGY	FAT	SAT FAT	PROTEIN	CARBS	SUGARS	SALT	FIBER
410kcal	18.8g	4.3g	15.5g	45.2g	9.1g	1.3g	3.4g

BAKED MUSHROOM SOUP

BREAD, SWEET RED ONIONS, GARLIC, THYME & GRUYÈRE

SERVES 4 | TOTAL 50 MINUTES

2 red onions

4 cloves of garlic

½ a bunch of thyme (½ oz)

10 oz mushrooms

10 oz good sourdough bread

4 cups fresh veg or chicken stock

2½ oz Gruyère cheese

Preheat the oven to 350°F. Peel and dice the onions, and peel and finely slice the garlic, then place in a large casserole pan on a medium-low heat with 1 tablespoon of olive oil. Strip in the thyme and cook for 10 minutes, stirring regularly, while you slice the mushrooms and tear the bread into 1½-inch chunks. Stir the mushrooms into the pan, pour in the stock and bring to a boil. Add the bread, then grate in most of the cheese. Stir well, grate over the remaining cheese and transfer to the oven for 25 minutes, or until dark golden and very thick. Season to perfection, then serve drizzled with extra virgin olive oil. Comfort in a bowl.

ENERGY	FAT	SAT FAT	PROTEIN	CARBS	SUGARS	SALT	FIBER
332kcal	10.7g	4.4g	16.1g	42g	6.9g	1g	2.9g

MUSHROOM CACIO E PEPE

CLASSIC PASTA WITH PECORINO CHEESE, SPIKED WITH TRUFFLE OIL & LEMON

SERVES 1 | **TOTAL 10 MINUTES**

2¾ oz dried spaghetti

1 oz pecorino or Parmesan cheese

2 chestnut or cremini mushrooms

½ teaspoon truffle oil

½ a lemon

Cook the pasta in a pan of boiling salted water according to the package instructions. Finely grate the cheese and 1 mushroom into a small bowl, then add the truffle oil, a squeeze of lemon juice and a couple of good pinches of black pepper. Add 2 tablespoons of pasta cooking water and mix together really well.

Drain the pasta, return to the pan, then beat in the mushroom mixture with a spatula. It should be shiny and not wet – intense in flavor and hot from the black pepper. Pour the pasta into your bowl and finely grate over the remaining raw mushroom, which will be fresh and nutty in flavor. Eat right away.

ENERGY	FAT	SAT FAT	PROTEIN	CARBS	SUGARS	SALT	FIBER
400kcal	12.8g	5.5g	18.5g	56.2g	3g	0.7g	2.4g

MUSHROOM & BEEF STIR-FRY

GIANT NOODLES, FRAGRANT GINGER, GARLIC, CHILI OIL, SOY & SCALLIONS

SERVES 2 | TOTAL 20 MINUTES

1 bunch of scallions

4 cloves of garlic

2½-inch piece of fresh ginger

4¼ oz fresh lasagne sheets

1 x 5¼-oz beef tenderloin

8 oz oyster mushrooms

1½ tablespoons chili oil

1½ tablespoons reduced-sodium
soy sauce

Trim the scallions and chop into 1¼-inch lengths. Peel and finely slice the garlic. Peel and matchstick the ginger. Slice the lasagne sheets into ¾-inch-thick noodles. Rub the steak with 1 teaspoon of olive oil, a small pinch of sea salt and a pinch of black pepper. Put a large non-stick frying pan on a high heat. Dry-fry the mushrooms for 3 minutes on one side only. Meanwhile, mix the chili oil, soy, 1 tablespoon of red wine vinegar and a pinch of black pepper in a large bowl. Tip the mushrooms straight into the bowl of dressing, returning the pan to the heat.

Cook the steak to your liking in the hot pan, turning every minute, with the scallions, garlic and ginger alongside, stirring them occasionally. Meanwhile, cook the pasta noodles in a pan of boiling salted water for 3 minutes. Remove just the steak to a board to rest for a moment, then use tongs to drag the noodles straight into the frying pan, letting a splash of pasta cooking water go with them. Remove from the heat, pour in the mushrooms and dressing and toss together. Divide between bowls, then thinly slice and add the steak, drizzling over any resting juices, to finish.

ENERGY	FAT	SAT FAT	PROTEIN	CARBS	SUGARS	SALT	FIBER
366kcal	18.5g	5.1g	24.5g	25.6g	3.5g	1.6g	1.7g

1 PEPPER-CRUSTED STEAK
CREAMY MUSTARD & WHISKY SAUCE, SIMPLE BROCCOLI

2 STICKY GINGER BEEF
CHILI JAM, RICE NOODLES, LIME, CUCUMBER & PEANUTS

3 SEARED STEAK & RED CHIMICHURRI
SMASHED SWEET POTATO, CHARRED SCALLIONS & CRISPY BITS

4 STEAK SANDWICH, JAPANESE-STYLE
WASABI, TANGY PICKLED CUCUMBER SALAD & TOASTED SESAME SEEDS

5 PROSCIUTTO & SAGE MINUTE STEAK
POTATO & CARROT RÖSTI, FRIED EGG & FRENCH-DRESSED SPINACH SALAD

6 JUICY SEARED STEAK
TOMATOES, ARTICHOKES, MINT, LEMON & FLUFFY COUSCOUS

7 BEEF WELLINGTON FOR 2
PUFF PASTRY, SPINACH PANCAKES & MUSHROOM PÂTÉ

STEAK

PEPPER-CRUSTED STEAK

CREAMY MUSTARD & WHISKY SAUCE, SIMPLE BROCCOLI

SERVES 2 | TOTAL 20 MINUTES

1 head of broccoli (13 oz)

1 large shallot

2 x 5¼-oz beef tenderloins

2 tablespoons Scotch whisky

1 heaping teaspoon Dijon mustard

7 tablespoons heavy cream

Trim the tough end off the broccoli stalk, use a vegetable peeler to remove the outer layer from the remaining stalk, then halve the head. Peel and finely chop the shallot. Place a large non-stick frying pan on a high heat. Rub the steaks with ½ a tablespoon of olive oil, a pinch of sea salt and plenty of black pepper, then put in the hot pan. Cook to your liking, turning every minute. In a medium pan, cook the broccoli in boiling salted water for 5 minutes.

Move the steaks to a plate to rest. Put the shallot straight into the hot pan with 1 tablespoon of oil. Stir and soften for 1 minute. Add the whisky and – if you want to – very carefully flame it. When the flame subsides, stir in the mustard, cream and a splash of water. Simmer for 1 minute, adding any steak resting juices to the mix. Plate up the broccoli and creamy sauce, slice and add the steak, then drizzle with 1 teaspoon of extra virgin olive oil, to finish.

ENERGY	FAT	SAT FAT	PROTEIN	CARBS	SUGARS	SALT	FIBER
493kcal	32.2g	12.5g	39.6g	6.2g	4.4g	1.3g	5.2g

STICKY GINGER BEEF

CHILI JAM, RICE NOODLES, LIME, CUCUMBER & PEANUTS

SERVES 2 | TOTAL 20 MINUTES

3 oz rice vermicelli noodles

½ an English cucumber

2½-inch piece of fresh ginger

1 romaine lettuce

2 limes

1 heaping tablespoon chili jam or red pepper jelly

1 x 7-oz sirloin steak

1 oz unsalted peanuts

In a heatproof bowl, cover the noodles with boiling kettle water. Finely slice the cucumber into batons. Peel and matchstick the ginger. Click apart the lettuce and finely shred the outer leaves, leaving the smaller inner leaves whole. Finely grate the zest of 1 lime into a bowl, squeeze in the juice, add half the chili jam and 1 tablespoon each of red wine vinegar and extra virgin olive oil to make a dressing. Drain and refresh the noodles, pile onto a platter with the lettuce and cucumber, pour over the dressing and toss well. Cut off and discard any fat and sinew from the steak, chop the steak into ¾-inch dice, then season with sea salt and black pepper.

Put a large non-stick frying pan on a high heat. Roughly chop the peanuts, toast for 3 minutes until golden, then put aside, returning the pan to the heat. Put ½ a tablespoon of olive oil and the ginger into the hot pan. Stir-fry for 1 minute, then toss in the steak for 1 minute – you don't want to overcook it. Stir in most of the peanuts and the remaining chili jam, then spoon the steak onto the platter, sprinkle over the remaining peanuts and serve with lime wedges, for squeezing over.

ENERGY	FAT	SAT FAT	PROTEIN	CARBS	SUGARS	SALT	FIBER
521kcal	22.2g	4.9g	31.8g	47.2g	8.5g	0.7g	2.3g

SEARED STEAK & RED CHIMICHURRI

SMASHED SWEET POTATO, CHARRED SCALLIONS & CRISPY BITS

SERVES 2 | TOTAL 20 MINUTES

1 x 9-oz sirloin steak

2 cloves of garlic

2 sweet potatoes (8 oz each)

1 bunch of scallions

2 fresh red chilies

½ x 16-oz jar of roasted red peppers

½ a bunch of Italian parsley (½ oz)

Remove and finely dice the fat from the steak. Put it into a non-stick frying pan on a medium-low heat with the unpeeled garlic cloves, turning them every minute in the fat as it gently crisps up. Meanwhile, peel the sweet potatoes and chop into 1½-inch chunks. Cook in boiling salted water for 10 minutes, or until tender, then drain, smash, season and keep warm. Trim the scallions, halve and seed the chilies, and lightly brown on both sides in the steak fat. Remove 4 scallions and the crispy fat bits to a dish, then place the rest of the scallions and the chilies in a blender and squeeze in the soft garlic flesh. Drain and add the peppers, along with the parsley and ½ a tablespoon each of extra virgin olive oil and red wine vinegar, then blitz until smooth, and season to perfection.

Turn the heat under the pan to high. Cut off the sinew, season the steak with sea salt and lots of black pepper, then cook to your liking, turning every minute. Let the steak rest for 1 minute on top of the scallions, then slice. Spoon 2 tablespoons of sauce onto each plate (save the rest for future meals), sit the steak on top with any resting juices, then serve with the sweet potato, scallions and crispy bits.

ENERGY	FAT	SAT FAT	PROTEIN	CARBS	SUGARS	SALT	FIBER
487kcal	17.1g	7.4g	32.7g	51.6g	11.4g	1.2g	7.6g

STEAK SANDWICH, JAPANESE-STYLE

WASABI, TANGY PICKLED CUCUMBER SALAD & TOASTED SESAME SEEDS

SERVES 1 | TOTAL 15 MINUTES

¼ of an English cucumber

1 teaspoon raw sesame seeds

1 x 5¼-oz lean sirloin steak

2 slices of soft bread

1 teaspoon wasabi paste

¾ oz watercress

Use a vegetable peeler to peel the cucumber, then finely slice into rounds. In a bowl, toss with a pinch of sea salt and 1 tablespoon of red wine vinegar, and leave to quickly pickle. In a non-stick frying pan, toast the sesame seeds until lightly golden, then remove. Cut off and discard any fat and sinew from the steak, then season the steak. Cook to your liking with a little olive oil on a high heat, turning every minute.

Spread the bread with wasabi paste (go hot or go home!), then add the steak, sandwich together and cut into fingers. Toss the watercress with the cucumber and sprinkle with the toasted sesame seeds, then serve.

ENERGY	FAT	SAT FAT	PROTEIN	CARBS	SUGARS	SALT	FIBER
497kcal	17.4g	5.9g	47.1g	37.1g	4.3g	1.7g	2.5g

PROSCIUTTO & SAGE MINUTE STEAK
POTATO & CARROT RÖSTI, FRIED EGG & FRENCH-DRESSED SPINACH SALAD

SERVES 1 | TOTAL 20 MINUTES

1 small potato (5¼ oz)

1 small carrot (3½ oz)

1 x 4½-oz minute steak

1 slice of prosciutto

1 sprig of sage

1 large egg

¼ teaspoon Dijon mustard

1 oz baby spinach

Wash the potato and carrot, then coarsely grate in long strokes. Toss with a pinch of sea salt, then place on a clean kitchen towel. Cut off and discard any fat and sinew from the steak, lay the prosciutto on top, press on the sage leaves, then pound with your fist to flatten and help them stick. Put 1 tablespoon of olive oil in a cold 12-inch non-stick frying pan. Squeeze the kitchen towel well to remove any excess liquid from the grated veg, then sprinkle evenly into the pan. Pat flat, place on a medium-high heat and cook for 5 minutes, or until crispy and golden. Carefully flip onto your plate and slide back into the pan to cook for another 3 minutes. Meanwhile, place a medium non-stick frying pan on a high heat. Rub the steak with 1 teaspoon of oil, fry for 2 minutes, prosciutto-side down, then flip for another minute, frying the egg to your liking alongside with a drizzle of oil.

Mix the mustard, a splash each of red wine vinegar and extra virgin olive oil and a little seasoning, then dress the spinach. Slide your edible rösti onto your plate, put the steak, fried egg and dressed spinach on top, and tuck in.

ENERGY	FAT	SAT FAT	PROTEIN	CARBS	SUGARS	SALT	FIBER
566kcal	26.1g	5.6g	49.9g	36.6g	6.4g	2.6g	5.7g

JUICY SEARED STEAK

TOMATOES, ARTICHOKES, MINT, LEMON & FLUFFY COUSCOUS

SERVES 2 | TOTAL 20 MINUTES

½ a bunch of mint (½ oz)

⅔ cup couscous

1 x 7-oz sirloin steak

¾ oz flaked almonds

½ tablespoon liquid honey

5½ oz ripe mixed-color cherry tomatoes

½ x 6-oz jar of artichoke hearts in oil

1 small preserved lemon

Pick the mint leaves. Pop the stalks into a bowl with the couscous, just cover with boiling kettle water, and cover. Cut off the sinew, season the steak with a small pinch of sea salt and a pinch of black pepper, then use tongs to stand it fat-side down in a large non-stick frying pan on a medium-high heat, turning it onto the flat sides once crisp and golden. Sear on each side, cooking to your liking – I like mine medium rare. Toast the almonds alongside for the last 30 seconds. Toss in the honey, then immediately remove the steak and almonds to a plate to rest.

Place the tomatoes in the hot pan, then drain and add the artichokes, along with a good splash of water. Fry and stir for 2 minutes while you finely chop the lemon, removing any seeds. Stir it into the pan with most of the mint leaves and cook for a few more minutes. Fluff up the couscous, season to perfection and divide between your plates, then spoon over the tomatoes and artichokes. Slice and add the steak, almonds, juices and all, then finish with the remaining mint leaves.

ENERGY	FAT	SAT FAT	PROTEIN	CARBS	SUGARS	SALT	FIBER
470kcal	16.9g	3.5g	34.4g	47.9g	8.8g	1.4g	7.1g

BEEF WELLINGTON FOR 2

PUFF PASTRY, SPINACH PANCAKES & MUSHROOM PÂTÉ

SERVES 2 | **TOTAL 1 HOUR 30 MINUTES**

1 red onion

8 oz mixed mushrooms

1 x 7¾-oz beef tenderloin

½ a bunch of thyme (½ oz)

2 large eggs

1 cup all-purpose flour,
plus extra for dusting

3½ oz baby spinach

1 x 11-oz sheet of all-butter
puff pastry (cold)

Peel the onion and roughly chop with the mushrooms. Put a 12-inch non-stick frying pan on a high heat. Season the beef with sea salt and plenty of black pepper and rub with 1 teaspoon of olive oil. Turning with tongs, sear the beef all over for 2 minutes in total, then remove to a plate. Return the pan to a medium heat with the onion and mushrooms. Strip in the thyme. Cook for 15 minutes, or until soft, stirring regularly. Blitz in a food processor until spreadable, season to perfection and remove. Blitz 1 egg, the flour, spinach, a pinch of salt and 1 cup of water in the processor until smooth. Put your pan back on a medium heat, rub with oil, then pour in a thin layer of batter. Cook for 1 minute on each side without coloring. Tip onto a plate to cool. Cover the leftover batter and chill for breakfast or brunch.

Preheat the oven to 425°F. Sit your pancake on a large sheet of plastic wrap. Evenly spread over the mushroom pâté. Place the beef in the center, then gather up the plastic wrap and twist into a parcel. Sit the pancake-wrapped beef (plastic wrap discarded) on the pastry, ¾ inch from one side. Eggwash all the pastry, then fold and mold the excess over the wrapped beef, leaving a pastry border around it. Trim to ¾ inch, pinch the edges to seal, eggwash and decorate with the trimmings, if you like. Cook at the bottom of the oven for 25 minutes, or until the pastry is golden on top and crispy underneath, for blushing, juicy beef. Rest for 2 minutes, then serve.

ENERGY	FAT	SAT FAT	PROTEIN	CARBS	SUGARS	SALT	FIBER
616kcal	34.1g	19g	33g	44.1g	7.3g	1.1g	5.5g

1 BEJEWELED BBQ PORK
GARLIC CHIPS, ROSEMARY, FLUFFY RICE & BEANS, TOMATOES & FRESH CHILI

2 PORK SCHNITZEL
BLUSHING POTATO SALAD & FRIED EGGS

3 PROSCIUTTO PORK TENDERLOIN
OOZY CHEESY GNOCCHI & PEA GRATIN, PESTO & CRISPY SAGE

4 PORK & BLACK BEAN SAUCE
RICE NOODLES, CRUNCHY VEG, FRESH CHILI, GARLIC & SHRIMP CHIPS

5 MY PORK VINDALOO
BUTTERNUT SQUASH, GARLIC, CURRY LEAVES & CHAPATIS

6 SWEET 'N' SOUR PORK
SHRIMP, CRUNCHY MIXED VEG, PEACHES & FLUFFY RICE

7 HOISIN PORK
GIANT SOFT STEAMED BUN, GARNISHES & SPRINKLES

PORK

BEJEWELED BBQ PORK

GARLIC CHIPS, ROSEMARY, FLUFFY RICE & BEANS, TOMATOES & FRESH CHILI

SERVES 2 | TOTAL 25 MINUTES

1 x 15-oz can of black beans

½ cup basmati rice

4 cloves of garlic

2 sprigs of rosemary

1 x 8-oz piece of pork tenderloin

8 oz ripe mixed-color cherry tomatoes

2 fresh red chilies

2 tablespoons BBQ sauce

Pour the beans into a medium pan on a medium-high heat, juice and all. Add ½ a cup of rice and 1 cup of boiling kettle water. Season with sea salt and black pepper, stir and cook uncovered for 12 minutes. Cover and turn the heat off.

Meanwhile, peel and finely slice the garlic, then cook in a non-stick frying pan on a medium-high heat with 1 tablespoon of olive oil, removing to a plate when lightly golden. Strip in the rosemary for 1 minute, removing once crispy. Trim the pork of any sinew, then cut into two chunky pieces and rub all over with pepper. Cook for 12 minutes, or until just cooked through, turning regularly, while you halve or quarter the cherry tomatoes, finely slice the chilies, season and mix with ½ a tablespoon each of red wine vinegar and extra virgin olive oil. Move the pork to a plate, spoon over the BBQ sauce, then bejewel with the crispy garlic and rosemary and leave to rest. Plate up the rice and beans, with the tomato salad on the side, and serve with the bejeweled pork.

ENERGY	FAT	SAT FAT	PROTEIN	CARBS	SUGARS	SALT	FIBER
434kcal	19.7g	4.7g	38.7g	20g	9.2g	1.6g	13.9g

PORK SCHNITZEL

BLUSHING POTATO SALAD & FRIED EGGS

SERVES 2 | TOTAL 20 MINUTES

20 oz canned new potatoes

1¾ oz mixed baby cornichons
   & pickled onions

¼ cup plain yogurt

1 heaping teaspoon Dijon mustard

2 jarred pickled baby beets

2 x 7-oz boneless pork loin chops

3 large eggs

½ cup fine dried breadcrumbs

Pour the potatoes, juice and all, into a small pan on a medium heat and boil for 3 minutes. Finely chop the cornichons and pickled onions and, in a large bowl, mix with the yogurt and mustard. Drain and stir in the potatoes, then season to perfection. Finely chop the beets and pile on top, ready to mix later.

Cut the fat off the pork chops and discard, then carefully slice through the middle of each pork chop with a sharp knife so you can open it out flat like a book, and flatten with your fist. Beat 1 egg in a shallow bowl, and spread the breadcrumbs across a plate. Season the pork, dip in the egg, letting any excess drip off, then turn in the breadcrumbs until well coated. Put a large non-stick frying pan on a medium-high heat with enough olive oil to coat the bottom of the pan. Once hot, add the pork chops and cook for 8 minutes, or until golden, turning halfway, then remove to a plate lined with paper towel to drain, leaving the pan on the heat. Quickly crack in the remaining eggs and fry to your liking, then drain those, too. Toss the potato salad, plate everything up, sprinkle over a pinch of black pepper and serve.

ENERGY	FAT	SAT FAT	PROTEIN	CARBS	SUGARS	SALT	FIBER
838kcal	49.2g	14.5g	49.1g	49.1g	7.8g	2.8g	2.5g

PROSCIUTTO PORK TENDERLOIN

OOZY CHEESY GNOCCHI & PEA GRATIN, PESTO & CRISPY SAGE

SERVES 4 | TOTAL 50 MINUTES

2 cups reduced-fat (2%) milk

2 oz Parmesan cheese

1 lb potato gnocchi

11 oz frozen peas

8 slices of prosciutto

2 tablespoons green pesto

1 x 1-lb piece of pork tenderloin

½ a bunch of sage (½ oz)

Preheat the oven to 425°F. Pour the milk into a blender, grate in most of the cheese, add just 10 pieces of gnocchi and a pinch of black pepper and blitz until smooth to make a sauce. Put the remaining gnocchi and the peas into a 10-inch non-stick ovenproof frying pan, place on a medium heat, pour over the sauce and bring to a boil. Meanwhile, lay out a 20-inch sheet of parchment paper, lay over the prosciutto slices side by side, slightly overlapping, then spread the pesto all over them. Trim the pork of any sinew, rub it all over with a pinch of black pepper, lay it across one end of the prosciutto and use the paper to help you roll it up, wrapping the pork in the prosciutto. Sit it on an oiled baking pan. Finely grate the remaining cheese over the gnocchi, then carefully transfer the pan to the oven. Place the pork at the bottom of the oven and cook both for 30 minutes.

About 5 minutes before the time is up, take the pork pan out of the oven and use the sage as a brush to baste the pork with the juices from the pan, then carefully tear the sage leaves over the pork and return to the oven for the remaining time. Remove to rest for 5 minutes, leaving the gnocchi in the oven, then serve the pork and gnocchi together, spooning any remaining pan juices over the pork.

ENERGY	FAT	SAT FAT	PROTEIN	CARBS	SUGARS	SALT	FIBER
674kcal	25.7g	9.4g	51.7g	59.1g	9g	2.8g	6.1g

PORK & BLACK BEAN SAUCE

RICE NOODLES, CRUNCHY VEG, FRESH CHILI, GARLIC & SHRIMP CHIPS

SERVES 2 | TOTAL 15 MINUTES

3 oz rice vermicelli noodles

1 onion

1 fresh red chili

1 x 8-oz piece of pork tenderloin

4 cloves of garlic

6 oz mixed baby corn & snowpeas

2 heaping tablespoons black
    bean sauce

¾ oz shrimp chips

Put a large non-stick frying pan on a high heat. In a heatproof bowl, cover the noodles with boiling kettle water. Peel the onion and chop into ½-inch chunks, roughly slice the chili, then dry-fry and char both in the hot pan for 2 minutes, stirring regularly. Trim the pork of any sinew, then chop it into ¾-inch chunks. Peel and slice the garlic, stir into the pan with the pork and 1 tablespoon of olive oil and stir-fry for 2 minutes. Chop the baby corn and snowpeas into ¾-inch lengths, then toss into the pan and stir-fry for another 2 minutes. Add 1 tablespoon of red wine vinegar and the black bean sauce, let it sizzle for 30 seconds, or until the pork is just cooked through, then season to perfection.

Drain the noodles and divide between your bowls. Spoon the pork, veg and black bean sauce on top, crumble over the shrimp chips and tuck in.

ENERGY	FAT	SAT FAT	PROTEIN	CARBS	SUGARS	SALT	FIBER
574kcal	19.8g	4.2g	34.9g	62.8g	9.8g	0.6g	2.8g

MY PORK VINDALOO

BUTTERNUT SQUASH, GARLIC, CURRY LEAVES & CHAPATIS

SERVES 4 | TOTAL 1 HOUR

½ a butternut squash (1¼ lbs)

2 onions

8 cloves of garlic

2 cups whole-grain self-rising flour

1 x 14-oz can of plum tomatoes

1 x 1-lb piece of pork tenderloin

20 curry leaves

2 heaping tablespoons Madras curry paste

Preheat the oven to 350°F. Peel the neck end of the squash and chop into ¾-inch dice. Peel the onions and chop the same size. Peel and halve the garlic cloves. Toss it all in a large shallow non-stick casserole pan with 1 tablespoon of olive oil and roast for 40 minutes. Meanwhile, pile the flour into a large bowl with a small pinch of sea salt, then gradually add ⅔ cup of water and mix into a dough. Knead on a flour-dusted surface for 2 minutes, then divide into 4 equal balls and roll out thinly. Dry-fry for 1 minute on each side in a non-stick frying pan on a high heat, then wrap in aluminum foil and, when you switch the oven off, pop the foil parcel in to keep warm.

Transfer the casserole pan to a medium-high heat on the stove. Pour in the tomatoes and 1 can's worth of water, breaking up the tomatoes with a spoon, then simmer for 10 minutes. Return the frying pan to a high heat alongside, then trim the pork of any sinew, chop into ¾-inch chunks and place in the pan with ½ a tablespoon of oil. Stir-fry for 5 minutes, then add the curry leaves, paste and ¼ cup of red wine vinegar, stirring for 1 minute until well coated and the pork is just cooked through. Tip it all into the squash pan, stir together well and season to perfection. Serve with the warm chapatis on the side.

ENERGY	FAT	SAT FAT	PROTEIN	CARBS	SUGARS	SALT	FIBER
566kcal	17g	3.5g	40.8g	66.6g	17.9g	1.8g	11.9g

SWEET 'N' SOUR PORK
SHRIMP, CRUNCHY MIXED VEG, PEACHES & FLUFFY RICE

SERVES 2 | **TOTAL 15 MINUTES**

½ cup basmati rice

1 x 10-oz package of mixed stir-fry veg

½ x 15-oz can of peach slices
   in juice

1 heaping tablespoon tomato &
   chili chutney

1 tablespoon reduced-sodium
   soy sauce

2 x 7-oz boneless pork loin chops

3 oz raw peeled jumbo shrimp

2 tablespoons cornstarch

Put ½ a cup of rice, 1 cup of boiling kettle water and a small pinch of sea salt into a small pan. Cover, and cook on a medium heat for 12 minutes, adding the stir-fry veg to steam for the last 2 minutes, covered, then turn the heat off.

Meanwhile, drain half the peach juice into a bowl, then stir in the chutney, soy and 1 tablespoon of red wine vinegar to make a sauce. Put a large non-stick frying pan on a high heat. Cut the fat off the pork chops and discard. Dice the pork into ¾-inch chunks, then toss with the shrimp and cornstarch until well coated. Put 1 tablespoon of olive oil into the hot pan, then add just the floured pork to stir-fry for 4 minutes. Sprinkle in the shrimp and stir-fry for 1 minute, then add the drained peaches and sauce. Let it bubble and simmer for 1 more minute, then turn the heat off and season to perfection. Fluff up the rice, divide between your plates with the mixed veg, then spoon over the sweet 'n' sour pork, shrimp and peaches.

ENERGY	FAT	SAT FAT	PROTEIN	CARBS	SUGARS	SALT	FIBER
791kcal	31.6g	10g	45.1g	86.6g	13.2g	1.6g	5.3g

HOISIN PORK
GIANT SOFT STEAMED BUN, GARNISHES & SPRINKLES

SERVES 4 | **TOTAL 25 MINUTES**

2 cups self-rising flour

1 x 1-lb piece of pork tenderloin

1 English cucumber

4 scallions

7 oz radishes

1 bibb lettuce

1 oz wasabi peas

¼ cup hoisin sauce

Pile the flour into a large bowl with a small pinch of sea salt. Mix in ⅔ cup of water, knead lightly on a flour-dusted surface for 2 minutes, then cover and leave to rest. Trim the pork of any sinew, then cut into two chunky pieces and rub all over with black pepper. Place in a 12-inch non-stick frying pan on a medium-high heat with 1 tablespoon of olive oil and cook for 15 minutes, or until just cooked through, turning regularly. Use a fork to scrape down the outside of the cucumber, then finely slice. Trim the scallions, then finely slice with the radishes. Wash the lettuce and click apart into cups. Crush the wasabi peas in a pestle and mortar.

Move the pork to a plate, leaving the pan on the heat. Evenly spoon the hoisin sauce over the pork and leave to rest. Pour ¼ inch of water into the hot pan. Lightly rub a large sheet of parchment paper with oil, sit the dough on top, gently pull and stretch it out to 12 inches, then lightly score into quarters. Trim the paper so you can sit both paper and dough inside the pan, place inside, cover and steam for 5 minutes, or until cooked through. Serve everything at the table.

ENERGY	FAT	SAT FAT	PROTEIN	CARBS	SUGARS	SALT	FIBER
515kcal	14.2g	4.1g	36.9g	62.3g	11.7g	1.8g	4.9g

A NOTE FROM JAMIE'S WONDERFUL NUTRITION TEAM

Our job is to make sure that Jamie can be super-creative, while also ensuring that all his recipes meet the guidelines we set. Every book has a different brief, and *7 Ways* is about arming you with loads of inspiration for every day of the week. 72% of the recipes fit into our everyday food guidelines – some are complete meals, but there'll be others that you'll need to balance out with what's lacking. For absolute clarity and so that you can make informed choices, we've presented easy-to-read nutrition info for each dish on the recipe page itself, giving you a fast access point to understand how to fit these recipes into your week.

Food is fun, joyful and creative – it gives us energy and plays a crucial role in keeping our bodies healthy. Remember, a nutritious, balanced diet and regular exercise are the keys to a healthier lifestyle. We don't label foods as "good" or "bad" – there's a place for everything – but encourage an understanding of the difference between nutritious foods for everyday consumption and those to be enjoyed occasionally. For more info about our guidelines and how we analyze recipes, please visit **jamieoliver.com/nutrition**.

Rozzie Batchelar – Senior Nutritionist, RNutr (food)

A BIT ABOUT BALANCE

Balance is key when it comes to eating well. Balance your plate right and keep your portion control in check, and you can be confident that you're giving yourself a great start on the path to good health. It's important to consume a variety of foods to ensure we get the nutrients our bodies need to stay healthy. You don't have to be spot-on every day – just try to get your balance right across the week. If you eat meat and fish, as a general guide for main meals you want at least 2 portions of fish a week, one of which should be oily. Split the rest of the week's main meals between brilliant plant-based meals, some poultry and a little red meat. An all-vegetarian diet can be perfectly healthy, too.

WHAT'S THE BALANCE?

The easiest way to balance your plate is to follow government guidelines, like these ones from the UK government's *Eatwell Guide*, which shows us what a healthy balance of foods looks like. Check out the percentages they recommend below, and think about the proportion of food on your plate.

THE FIVE FOOD GROUPS (UK)	PROPORTION*
Vegetables and fruit	39%
Starchy carbohydrates (bread, rice, potatoes, pasta)	37%
Protein (lean meat, fish, eggs, beans, other non-dairy sources)	12%
Dairy foods, milk & dairy alternatives	8%
Unsaturated fats (such as oils)	1%
AND DON'T FORGET TO DRINK PLENTY OF WATER, TOO	

*Please note: the remaining 3% is made up of food to be enjoyed occasionally.

VEGETABLES & FRUIT

To live a good, healthy life, vegetables and fruit should sit right at the heart of your diet. Veg and fruit come in all kinds of colors, shapes, sizes, flavors and textures, and contain different vitamins and minerals, which each play a part in keeping our bodies healthy and optimal, so variety is key. Eat the rainbow, mixing up your choices as much as you can and embracing the seasons so you're getting produce at its best and its most nutritious. As an absolute minimum, aim for at least 5 portions of fresh, frozen or canned veg and fruit every day of the week, enjoying more wherever possible. 80g (or a large handful) counts as one portion. You can also count one 30g portion of dried fruit, one 80g portion of beans or pulses, and ⅔ cup of unsweetened veg or fruit juice per day.

STARCHY CARBOHYDRATES

Carbs provide us with a large proportion of the energy needed to make our bodies move, and to ensure our organs have the fuel they need to function. When you can, choose fiber-rich whole-grain and whole-wheat varieties. 260g is the recommended daily amount of carbohydrates for the average adult, with up to 90g coming from total sugars, which includes natural sugars found in whole fruit, milk and milk products, and no more than 30g of free sugars. Free sugars are those added to food and drink, including sugar found in honey, syrups, fruit juice and smoothies. Fiber is classified as a carbohydrate and is mainly found in plant-based foods such as whole-grain carbohydrates, veg and fruit. It helps to keep our digestive systems healthy, control our blood-sugar levels and maintain healthy cholesterol levels. Adults should be aiming for at least 30g each day.

PROTEIN

Think of protein as the building blocks of our bodies – it's used for everything that's important to how we grow and repair. Try to vary your proteins and include vegetarian sources. With animal-based proteins, choose lean cuts where you can, limit processed meat and aim to eat at least two portions of fish each week, one of which should be oily. The requirement for an average woman aged 19 to 50 is 45g per day, with 55g for men in the same age bracket.

DAIRY FOODS, MILK & DAIRY ALTERNATIVES

This food group offers an amazing array of nutrients when eaten in the right amounts. Favor organic milk and yogurt, and small amounts of cheese in this category; the lower-fat varieties (with no added sugar) are equally brilliant and worth embracing. If opting for plant-based versions, I think it's great that we have choice, but please don't be under the illusion that nutritionally you're swapping one milk for another. To bridge the gap to what is essentially flavored water, please look for a fortified, unsweetened option.

UNSATURATED FATS

While we only need small amounts, we do require healthier fats. Choose unsaturated sources where you can, such as olive and liquid vegetable oils, nuts, seeds, avocado and omega-3-rich oily fish. Generally speaking, it's recommended that the average woman has no more than 70g of fat per day, with less than 20g of that from saturated fat, and the average man no more than 90g, with less than 30g from saturates.

DRINK PLENTY OF WATER

To be the best you can be, stay hydrated. Water is essential to life, and to every function of the human body! In general, females aged 14 and over need at least 2 liters per day and males in the same age bracket need at least 2.5 liters per day.

ENERGY & NUTRITION INFO

The average woman needs 2,000 calories a day, while the average man needs roughly 2,500. These figures are a rough guide, and what we eat needs to be considered in relation to factors like age, build, lifestyle and activity levels.

THANK YOU

I've written a lot of thanks pages over the years and it never gets any easier, because there really are a lot of wonderful people, both within my business and beyond, who contribute either to the actual making of the book, or to the amazing support network that builds around it. It's impossible for me to name-check every one of these special beings here, so I've tried to keep it fairly short and sweet this year. If your name isn't here and you know you've played a part, then seek me out – I owe you a beer!

First up, as always, to my world-class food team. I am so grateful to have such a fantastic bunch of people sharing the food love on a daily basis. To the one and only Ginny Rolfe, and the rest of the amazing gang, Maddie Rix, Jodene Jordan, Elspeth Allison, Rachel Young, Hugo Harrison, Sharon Sharpe, Becky Merrick, Lydia Lockyer and Helen Martin, and to our extended food team family, freelancers Isla Murray, Sophie Mackinnon and Francesca Paling. To my long-standing food wives, Pete Begg and Bobby Sebire, I don't know if you're my work wives, you're each other's work wives, or we're all in it together. Whichever way, I'm grateful!

To my outstanding nutrition and technical teams – you keep me in check, I keep you in check, and together we're a force to be reckoned with. Special mention on this project must go to Rozzie "the batch" Batchelar and Lucinda Cobb.

On those all-important words, big love to my favorite vegetarian and Editor-in-Chief Rebecca Verity, to new girl in the mix, Editorial Assistant Jade Melling, and to the rest of the team.

Much gratitude to Levon Biss, our photographer for this one. I know it's the first time you've worked with food and I'm not sure you'll do it again, but it's been a pleasure. I love the energy and life you've brought to these pages. Shout out to assistant Mr. Richard Clatworthy – lots of love dude, and to lovely ladies Lima O'Donnell and Julia Bell.

Representing on the design front, big up to my mate James Verity at creative agency Superfantastic. You're still fast and you're still funky – thanks for being at the heart of the team and always mucking in.

EVERYONE!

To my publishers, the illustrious team at Penguin Random House. I'm sure you all, like me, have worked on this book with our dear late John Hamilton in mind, considering decisions through his lens. You know I love you all dearly, I genuinely want to hug you, and I am always grateful for your support and friendship. To Tom Weldon, Louise Moore, Elizabeth Smith, Clare Parker, Ella Watkins, Juliette Butler, Katherine Tibbals, Lee Motley, Sarah Fraser, Nick Lowndes, Christina Ellicott, Rachel Myers, Katie Corcoran, Natasha Lanigan, El Beckford, Louise Blakemore, Chantal Noel, Vanessa Forbes, Catherine Wood, Joshua Crosley, Jane Kirby, Lee-Anne Williams, Jade Unwin, Chris Wyatt, Tracy Orchard, Jane Delaney, Anna Curvis, Catherine Knowles. Also to our faithful freelancers, lovely Annie Lee, Sophie Elletson, Emma Horton and Caroline Wilding.

On to the rest of the business my side. I am lucky to be surrounded by brilliant people every day and I never take that for granted. Every team goes above and beyond and I'm so thankful for it. Pulling out those closest to the production and promotion of this book, I must thank my marketing and PR teams, Jeremy Scott, Katie McNeilage, Rosalind Godber, Michelle Dam, Saskia Wirth and Heather Milner. My excellent Head of Social, Subi Gnanaseharam, and her team. Our great leader, my brother-in-law CEO, Mr. Paul Hunt; my Deputy, Louise Holland; my Chief Content Officer, Zoe Collins; Group Head of Production, Sean Moxhay; and my legendary Executive Assistant, Ali Solway. And to all the other teams in the business, I love you all!

On the TV side, I'm thankful to work with a bunch of legends. Make sure you check out the show to see them all credited for the brilliant jobs they do. Big love to Sam Beddoes and Katie Millard, to their wonderful teams and the amazing crew. To my Channel 4 family and the Fremantle posse – thank you.

And to finish up, my beautiful family. You keep me sane (most of the time). Thank you for your constant love, support and encouragement. To my darling Jools, our motley crew, Poppy, Daisy, Buddy, Petal and little River, to my dear Mum and Dad, my sister Anna-Marie, and to Mrs. Norton and Leon. Last but never least, Mr. Gennaro Contaldo – you da best!

INDEX

Recipes marked V are suitable for vegetarians; in some instances you'll need to swap in a vegetarian alternative to cheeses such as Parmesan. (Some ground meat and sausage recipes can also be made with vegetarian alternatives; these are marked with ✳.)

T

For a quick reference list of all the vegetarian, vegan, dairy-free and gluten-free recipes in this book, please visit:

jamieoliver.com/7ways/reference

BOOKS BY JAMIE OLIVER

HUNGRY FOR MORE?

For handy nutrition advice, as well as videos, features, hints, tricks and tips on all sorts of different subjects, loads of brilliant recipes, plus much more, check out

JAMIEOLIVER.COM   #JAMIES7WAYS

Photography copyright © 2020 Levon Biss

Recipe photography by Levon Biss

© 2007 P22 Underground Pro Demi, All Rights Reserved P22 type foundry, Inc.

Dedication page photography by James Mooney

Designed by Superfantastic

Color reproduction by Altaimage Ltd

jamieoliver.com
www.flatironbooks.com

The Library of Congress Cataloging-in-Publication Data is available upon request.

ISBN 978-1-250-78757-6 (paper over board)
ISBN 978-1-250-78758-3 (ebook)

Our books may be purchased in bulk for promotional, educational, or business use. Please contact your local bookseller or the Macmillan Corporate and Premium Sales Department at 1-800-221-7945, extension 5442, or by email at MacmillanSpecialMarkets@macmillan.com.

Originally published in the United Kingdom in 2020 by Michael Joseph, an imprint of Penguin Books Ltd., part of the Penguin Random House group of companies.

Printed in Italy by Graphicom

First U.S. Edition: 2020

10 9 8 7 6 5 4 3 2 1